FINDING
HOPE

After the Devastating Loss
of Beloved Children

Dr. Doug & BJ Jensen

© 2011 Dr. Doug and BJ Jensen
11139 Morning Creek Dr. So.
San Diego, CA 92128
jensen2@san.rr.com

Edited by Peggy Hamerly at peghamerly@gmail.com.

Graphics & Layout by Carrie Fossati at CF Designs
- cfdesigns@cox.net.

Photo on Back Cover by Crystal Pridmore at Pridmoria Productions
- crystal@pridmoria.com.

Scripture verses are quoted from the New International Version
of the Bible.

Printed in the United States of America by Shadow Mountain
Printing, El Cajon, CA.

DEDICATION

This book is dedicated to "everyone who is in the club where no one wants to be a member" – parents who have experienced the death of a child or children. Writing this is our way to thank those of you who were able to comfort our healing journey because of your first-hand knowledge. You are the ones who walked the heartbreaking path ahead of us. We are grateful for your support and encouragement which helped us survive. Thank you for encouraging us to become a witness and inspiration to the other unfortunate grieving parents who follow.

Our heartfelt gratitude to the wonderful people at:

- **COMPASSIONATE FRIENDS**
  www.thecompassionatefriends.com
  (Parents, relatives, and friends of a child who died)
- **UMBRELLA MINISTRIES**
  www.umbrellaministries.com
  (Mothers helping other mothers who have also experienced the death of a child)
- **T.A.P.S. www.taps.org**
  (Tragedy Assistance Program for Survivors – for military families of the fallen)
- **S.O.S.L.** National website for suicide survivors: www.survivorsofsuicide.com
  (Survivors of Suicide Loss in San Diego)
- **GRIEFSHARE** www.griefshare.com
  (Grief Recovery Support Groups for the loss of a loved one)

INTRODUCTION

No one expects to experience what many consider the greatest possible loss – the death of a beloved child. The pain is so great it cannot be described with pen and paper. It cannot be expressed in eloquent speech. It can only be fully understood in shared experiences with others with similar stories.

We share our stories of loss and the stories of others, certainly not because we chose to rehash or be reminded of traveling those treacherous waters again. We write this book because you may feel like you are drowning in an ocean of tears right now and we felt called to pass on the lifelines we received. Ironically, it is in remembering and expressing the sometimes embarrassing details of our journey toward healing that our hearts are once again touched by those who cried with us, comforted us, and acted like an anchor in our most challenging moments.

Reading a book on grief may seem depressing, but it can also be uplifting. We can gain new insights and perspectives from the stories of those who have gone through similar experiences and not only survived the overwhelming grief, but have gone on to make a difference in the lives of others, in spite of their own devastating personal loss.

This book was written for those who are struggling to make sense out of the senseless, to lend a helping hand to those who find themselves in the pit of despair, and to give hope to the ones who feel hopeless.

We are all on a life journey that has been changed forever by loss. We didn't choose it; we didn't deserve it; we don't agree with it, but it is our new reality. It will take time to heal from the overwhelming blow that sent us reeling. Our life journey will never be the same. We have been forced to continue in a different direction, but it is possible to find a path that leads to hope and significant meaning. Many others have, and you can too.

May God bless us all as we seek a new direction.

TABLE OF CONTENTS

Part 1

Experiencing
The Horrible

"A wife who loses a husband is called a widow.
A husband who loses a wife is called a widower.
A child who loses his parents is called an orphan.
But there is no word for a parent, a step parent
or a grandparent who loses a child.
That's how awful the loss is."

- Unknown Author

1
Suffering
Losses

1967

The minimal bleeding persisted. After a few weeks, I became concerned enough to contact my gynecologist. No, this wasn't normal for me. No, I didn't feel sick. Yes, there was a good possibility I might be pregnant. I certainly was hoping for a baby girl to complete our family. Jeff and Jay were already two and four years old and they would be delighted with a baby sister to tease. My motherly instinct told me I was very pregnant.

But something wasn't quite right.

After my appointment, the doctor's office sent my urine specimen to the lab to determine whether I truly was pregnant. Today's pregnancy tests are able to detect the presence of the hormone hCG (secreted by the placenta immediately after a fertilized egg implants in the uterus and which shows up in both urine and blood) quickly and accurately.

In my hometown of Kankakee, Illinois in the 1960's, a patient's urine, containing the then unknown hormone hCG, would be injected into a baby rabbit to determine whether a patient was pregnant. The problem was that this method of testing required the soft, furry bunny to sacrifice his life if the test yielded a positive result. Unfortunately, the results were not always accurate and, luckily, during the "rabbit era" of pregnancy testing, this method was not popular or widespread. If my test bunny lived, it would mean I was not pregnant. Ironically, if the ill-fated bunny died, I would have the joy of knowing a new life was growing inside me. I hated to think about my being responsible for the death of anything, let alone a harmless and cuddly baby bunny.

After a few days of anxious anticipation, my pregnancy test results came back to reveal ... the rabbit lived. The pregnancy test was ... negative??? But that seemed impossible to me. I knew my body. I knew something was different. I started second guessing my certainty about whether I was pregnant.

The bleeding persisted, however, so I made another appointment with the gynecologist. Same questions. Same test. Same result! Probably the same live bunny continuing to enjoy life. My doctor now strongly recommended complete bed rest until the bleeding stopped.

I did. It didn't!

Lower abdominal pains and cramping sent me back to my obstetrician a third and a fourth time. Still shaking his head in a quandary, the only recommendation he could give me was invasive, exploratory abdominal surgery, the thought of which left me very frightened!

By this time, I knew in my heart I was pregnant with a baby girl. Don't ask me how I knew when the rabbits didn't. I just knew. I reasoned I was one-third of the way to having a beautiful daughter and was already anticipating the cute little pink bows and frilly pink polka dotted curtains.

4

Fear of harming or losing my long-awaited baby daughter and aversion to the prospect of pain and a slow recovery made me argue against the procedure. The doctor assured me he would do everything possible to save the baby ... if there were one. He added that the pain would be masked with medication and would eventually take care of itself.

But does pain ever "take care of itself?" Doesn't it require a decision or desire to endure the suffering for a time with the trust and hope that the future will be better?

At this point, the doctor told me that his main concern was finding the cause of the abnormal bleeding and stopping it. He also said that failure to do so could eventually lead to my death. He had my attention. I reluctantly submitted to the scalpel.

When I awoke following surgery, the results were gently revealed to me. They had removed one ovary AND a twelve-week-old fetus that was growing in my right fallopian tube. The doctor said he hadn't seen anything like it in all of his forty years of practice. I had presented the OB/GYN community a most unusual ectopic pregnancy specimen.

A normal pregnancy begins with a fertilized egg which travels to the uterus and attaches itself to the lining. In an ectopic ("out of place") pregnancy, the fertilized egg implants somewhere other than in the uterus. Since a fertilized egg needs the rich nourishment provided by the uterus to survive, an ectopic pregnancy cannot proceed normally. The growing tissue seeks sustenance wherever it has implanted itself by destroying surrounding maternal structures. A fallopian tube doesn't have as much space or nurturing tissue as a uterus does for a fetus to develop. But, untreated, the fetus continues to grow until it eventually ruptures the tube and causes severe pain and internal bleeding – a life-threatening situation leading to the mother's death in a matter of hours, even though the mother may be totally unaware of the pregnancy.

In my case, the egg implanted itself in my right fallopian tube. The tube had ruptured sometime previously. However, because it had attached itself to my nearby appendix, the fetus continued to get nourishment and grow. This also slowed down the rate of bleeding, masking the presence of a ruptured fallopian tube, and producing negative pregnancy test results. The surgical team had to remove all involved tissue. I was told it would be preserved for future medical study. My chances of becoming pregnant again were not good. I was told I was one of the lucky ones to survive.

At that point, I didn't see it that way.

"Blah, blah, blah" was all I heard after they said my baby was dead. I was crushed. I longed to slip back under the effects of the anesthetic and sleep forever.

Losing a much desired pregnancy is devastating, no matter what the reason, no matter whether you've only known about the pregnancy for a few days, a few weeks or, in my case, a few months. I had to face my loss and grieve for my unborn baby ... alone. My husband laughed at both my physical and emotional pain and readily admitted he was relieved we had lost the baby since he hadn't wanted another mouth to feed in the first place. I was physically and emotionally demoralized. It was one agonizingly slow day after another, suffering my sorrow in silence.

Fast forward through the drawn-out contested divorce from an emotionally and sometimes physically abusive husband. I believed marriage was a life-long commitment and that I would spend the rest of my life with him. So I found myself reeling from yet another unanticipated loss – that of a happy marriage. I made the decision to look forward in my life and vowed to NEVER remarry, thus avoiding any possible further losses.

We moved from Illinois, where all my family and friends lived, to the unknown - Southern California. It was as far as we could go to get away from an ex-husband who continued to stalk and threaten me while we lived in my hometown. It was the start of a new chapter in our lives, of believing that our share of shocking losses was behind and that the future would shine brighter. Jeff, Jay, and I were determined to think of it as an exciting adventure. I did not anticipate the grieving we experienced after relocating and losing the daily presence of the family and friends we left behind. So much for never having to suffer again!

In an imperfect world, suffering is an unavoidable part of the human condition. Fortunately, hope is also a part of the human condition.

2
Sharing
Experiences

BJ's Story

I was born and raised in Kankakee, Illinois and was a teen-age bride. My former husband and I had two sons. Jeff, the oldest, was the meticulous, disciplined, studious, and easy-to-reason-with son. He was well respected and liked by a select few whom he allowed into his small circle of friends. Our youngest son, John Jay, was the happy-go-lucky type who lived life to the fullest. His main goal was to have a good time. He had a quick smile and a contagious laugh. Jay enjoyed and looked forward to the next adventure, thrill, or challenge. His easy-going, fun-loving nature attracted many loving friends.

But all was not perfect in this imperfect world. The world saw a happy, thriving young family. But behind closed doors a different picture developed.

When their father was sober, he was an enjoyable person. However, when he wasn't sober, which occurred with increasing frequency, he became extremely nasty. When Jeff and Jay were preteens, they came to me and tearfully pleaded for the three of us to divorce their daddy because they were so afraid of his wild mood swings, his drunken binges followed by physical and verbal abuse, and his erratic behavior that threatened all of our lives. They realized before anything unspeakable happened and for the sake of everyone's safety, it was time to leave. So, after the agonizing divorce, Jeff, Jay, and I moved to a new state to start a new life, far away from the pain of the past.

For twelve years, I took my role as a single parent seriously. This sometimes overwhelming job for one person had many rewards. Jeff, Jay, and I became a close threesome. I really reveled in seeing our sweet little munchkins grow into responsible young men. In what seemed like "no time," they were off attending a local college and university.

Once Jeff and Jay had embarked on their exploration of a higher education, I was perfectly satisfied to turn most of my time and attention from raising the loves of my life to concentrating on and building a successful career as The Director of Health and Physical Education for the San Diego Downtown YMCA. My YMCA career in the health and fitness field had started part time in Illinois and spanned twenty years.

The sum total of my disappointment in and life-threatening experiences with my former husband gave me a profound distrust of men and firmly convinced me that I definitely did NOT want to remarry. However, God had other plans – a theme that has often repeated itself in my life.

Doug's Story

BJ and I met at the singles group in our church. I had never been married and wanted very much to marry, settle down, and raise a family. The problem was that, up to that point in my life, all of my relationships with potential marriage partners had ended unsuccessfully. I decided to give up my search for a life partner.

My relationship with BJ started out simply as friends enjoying being part of our church's social group. As we got to know each other, under no pressure, we found we had a great deal in common. We shared similar religious values; each had a quirky sense of humor, and joyful spirits which laughed easily with one another. In addition, we could communicate on an intellectual level. We both were athletic, enjoying sports like tennis, volleyball, and co-ed softball. We enjoyed feeling an easy-going, unforced, comfortable pleasure in each other's company.

Soon, a serious relationship blossomed and continued to grow. Eleven months after meeting, Doug proposed and I surprised myself by saying YES! Was that me or God talking? Jeff and Jay did not share our enthusiasm. They were very protective of their mom, and didn't want her to remarry.

With reluctant approval, her sons decided they would not give BJ away, but that they would share her with me. They agreed to walk their mom down the aisle. They saw my sincerity, love, and respect in the way I treated their mom.

Jeff and Jay - BJ's Story

Jay is our youngest of two highly intelligent and handsome sons. (But then, what mother doesn't think that of her sons?) Jay was especially gifted when it came to math. For example, when he was only five years old, he added, subtracted, multiplied, and divided - in double figures.

One night, as the three of us washed and dried the dishes the old fashioned way – by hand, (these were the good 'ole days before we had that modern convenience called a dishwasher) Jeff casually inquired how long it would take him to save his dishwashing allowance of fifteen cents per week to buy a G.I. Joe action figure. Without hesitation, Jay responded with the exact number of weeks to the complicated problem, that is, if you account for the tax. Jeff and I were both taken aback by what seemed like a speedy offhanded prediction.

"Is that right, mom?" disbelieving Jeff wanted to know. Taking up a pen and paper, I scribbled out the tricky math problem. Jay was absolutely correct.

"How did you do that, Jay? How did you figure that out?" I questioned.

"I don't know," offered Jay so innocently. "It was just in my head."

Jay was a tow-headed blond from birth and grew into his strikingly muscled physique and manly good looks. When he walked into a room, the room lit up with his joy, energy, and enthusiasm. His hobbies involved all aspects of sports from watching them to participating in them, from fantasy sports games, to the sport of romping on the sunny San Diego beaches with Cabo, his beloved Siberian Husky.

Jay was a top-level real estate appraiser at Bank of America where his math skills came in handy on high-end appraisals. He drove a sporty BMW convertible and lived on prestigious Coronado Island in San Diego.

A Growing Family?

After our wedding and only five months of wedded stress, trying to meld our different thoughts, needs, and wants, Doug and I had inklings that we were pregnant! How excitedly we anticipated the stork's arrival with a new bundle for our newly feathered nest! We hoped this good news might help smooth the rough edges we experienced in our adjustment to married life.

However, the suspected pregnancy turned out instead to be a tumor in my uterus that warranted a complete hysterectomy (removal of the uterus) and oophorectomy (removal of my remaining fallopian tube and ovary). There was no more possibility of having children together. To say we were devastated is an understatement! It was the death of a dream for the future. The finality of infertility seemed like a death sentence. Our marriage would not be blessed with biological children. I felt the overwhelming desperation that biblical wives Sarah, Rebecca, and Rachel must have felt over 4,000 years ago... I couldn't conceive or give birth to the sons and daughters my husband longed for. It was the most crushing news we could have been given at that time in our relationship. Instead of a newborn helping us adjust to marriage, this dreadful news caused even more stress.

After our dark and depressing time of grieving over my infertility, we began to consider the possibility of adoption.

We answered a city-wide plea from Child Adoptive Services for prospective adoptive parents. Although there were many infants needing loving homes, we were turned away because we were considered too old to start a family. We were told to try adopting an older or hard-to-adopt child. When we did, we were told we might be better suited to try adopting a newborn, etc. etc.   We knew we could provide a great home for any child, but one door after another on the adoption front slammed in our hopeful faces.   All of our many attempts at adoption failed.   We saw the run-around as another severe and devastating blow to a newly married couple wanting to raise a young family.

There was, however, a glimmer of hope on the horizon.   A young unmarried relative was dealing with an unexpected pregnancy.   We offered to adopt her baby.   The mommy-to-be agreed that ours would be a welcomed solution to her dilemma.   We were elated!   After the home birth of her beautiful daughter, the awe-struck mommy changed her mind.   Her heart told her that she needed to keep and raise her baby as a single parent.   We were genuinely happy for her and so sad for ourselves.   The deflating disappointment led us to vent our pent-up anger at God and at each other.   We couldn't understand what God was doing.   Why was He denying us the opportunity to be blessed with a baby?   We knew we could be awesome parents.

In hindsight, we saw how we needed to concentrate on our own personal growth and on building a stronger marriage.   With time, we gained new focus and direction.   We found a niche working side-by-side and helping other couples who were struggling in their marriages.   Had we been focused on raising our family, we wouldn't have had as much time to support as many couples as we did over the years.

Fast forward 10 years.

On a sunny warm day in August 1995, I (BJ) was home alone.   Doug was at an all-day seminar in Los Angeles, two hours north of our home in San Diego.   We didn't own cell phones at the time so we knew we would be out of contact with each other for the day. Our oldest son Jeff was now grown and living and working in Brawley, two hours east of San Diego.

The doorbell rang. I experienced a dreadful foreboding even before I opened the door to the two police detectives. They asked to come in. They asked to sit down. I didn't understand their solemn demeanor. They asked me to "have a seat." They reluctantly unveiled what seemed to me a bizarre story, so unbelievable that I was confused. They informed me that our youngest son, Jay, had just jumped to his death off the 200-foot tall Coronado Bay Bridge. I thought they had made a mistake. They hadn't.

The news slammed me in the face like an anvil. My mind went reeling and blank. It was fortunate that I was sitting or I would have fallen. I was totally shocked, horrified, and still in disbelief. It couldn't be happening a third time! First, the crushing blow of the death of an unborn fetus, then a second painful strike with the loss of fertility, and now, the knock out punch - the death of a precious child.

Since the rest of my family was out of town, the officers stayed with me until I could reach our pastor and friends and ask them to come to our house to be with me. I am grateful they didn't leave me alone. Pastor John, with two good church friends came to offer comfort until Jeff and his future wife, Monica, arrived. Several hours later Doug returned home from LA. Everything seemed to be moving like a slow motion picture as my mind and body slipped in and out of shock.

On the outside, Jay's life had been the picture of health and success. What we didn't know at the time of his shocking death, was that on the inside, he was engaged in fighting personal demons, in a life and death struggle on the battle-ground of his mind. We were told, after the fact, that it's a similar battle that other undiagnosed manic depressive people fight. And, like Jay, sometimes lose.

If only we had known about mental illness at the time!

Alan Pedersen, father of vibrant 18-year-old Ashley who died in a tragic car accident, says there is complicated grief that some parents have to deal with when death comes so quickly and unexpectedly. Other situations which can complicate the grieving process and keep us from moving through our grief are: a violent death, a murder, a suicide, finding the body of our loved one, trauma from deaths that were wit-nessed, legal issues, estranged relationships, divorces and custody of surviving children and grandchildren. We agree.

Whatever the circumstances surrounding the death of a child, be it disease, accident, criminal action, S.I.D.S. (sudden infant death syndrome), suicide, or some other means, there are questions that arise. Why my child? Why now? Why before my death? Why did they have to suffer? Why didn't they have a chance for a long, productive and happy life? Why didn't I know so I could have prevented this from happening? And the list of "whys" goes on.

Questions are inevitable; answers are not; at least not right away, perhaps never. Unresolved issues in the mind can lead to despair, to depression, and to hopelessness.

Jay found himself in a position he considered hopeless. He could not see any options out of the dark hole that was enveloping him. He did have options, but he could not see them and didn't know how to ask for guidance to get through the maze.

We do not want anyone to experience hopelessness. There are options, even when life appears hopeless. Through our devastating experiences as a parent and a step parent after the death of our son John Jay, we seek to offer hope, help, and healing to those who may be newly bereaved as well as to those parents, step parents, grandparents, other family members, and their friends who may travel this difficult path.

3
Sacrificing as a
Spouse or Step Parent

Voice of a Step Parent - Doug's Perspective

Little did I realize the rocky road we would travel when I married into a ready-made family. It was a journey we didn't plan to go on; a journey we didn't want to go on; a journey we wouldn't wish for anyone to take - the overwhelmingly heartbreaking journey of grieving the death of a beloved child.

On that fateful August night, the instant I walked in the front room and saw my wife, our eldest son Jeff and his fiancée Monica, I sensed the heaviness in the air and knew that something was terribly wrong. Today, I still have that image emblazoned in my memory - all three of them huddled together and me standing alone at the front door. At that moment, I felt like an intruder who had mistakenly stumbled into a secret meeting, an outsider peering into a family's private circle of grief.

In retrospect, it is easy to see why I felt like an outsider: I hadn't yet been informed about the tragedy. BJ, Jeff, and Monica were seated together holding each other while I stood at the front door – twenty feet away. Their extreme torment was evident but I was completely clueless about the situation. They had been grieving for hours; I was just now entering into that surrealistic "twilight zone" that occurs when learning tragic news.

I am grateful that BJ and Jeff didn't minimize the impact it would make on me as Jay's step dad or leave me outside of the family circle. In my opinion, they did a beautiful and loving thing when they opened their arms to include me in their grieving circle, treating me like a birth parent as they hugged me, cried with me, listened to me, answered my questions, and soothed my tears as I, too, wept for Jay. They understood my need to express my broken heart and to be comforted in the gauntlet of grief. Many step parents have labeled themselves as "the overlooked" or "the left out" mourner. I did not feel that way now.

Death, Grief, and Hopelessness

A common component of hopelessness is feeling all alone; feeling and thinking that no one understands the depth and pain of my grief. You think no one can help you escape the dark pit of sorrow. These thoughts and feelings actually can become self-fulfilling, separating us from family and friends who want to walk through the valley with us. They may be holding out a hand of hope, a hug of comfort, or a shoulder to cry on.

In the first days, weeks, months, and sometimes years after the death of our child, we can't feel or think about anything. We just experience the crushing pain of grief. As time passes, windows of opportunity open and we begin to communicate about our pain with our closest loved ones or friends. It is then we also begin to see their grief, which may be expressed very differently from ours.

Supporting Each Other - BJ's Perspective

Everyone who experiences the death of a child grieves in different ways. EVERYONE! Men grieve differently than women do. Parents grieve differently than siblings. Step parents grieve differently than birth parents. So much depends on how long a person knew the child who died and the extent of their relationship.

In addition to personally grieving Jay's death, Doug made a conscious decision that one of his primary roles was to support me in my grief journey. Since he works out of our home, he would be there for me unless appointments called him away. He chose to do whatever it would take to love me through my grief... no matter how long it took. I had given birth to Jay; he was an important part of my very being, and he had been senselessly ripped away. I felt like I had experienced serious major surgery ... WITHOUT ANESTHETIC.

What a challenge it was for Doug because we grieved very differently. While I had great difficulty getting to sleep at night, reliving the tragic death scene over and over, Doug would fall asleep as soon as his head hit the pillow. Every morning, he would awake with abundant energy, ready to get up and get going, while I awoke crying and wailing uncontrollably, unable to even crawl out of bed. At those times, Doug chose to simply stay in bed with me and hold me in his arms until my sobbing subsided. This was no small sacrifice because it happened over and over, every single day for months.

As the first year after Jay's death passed, the length of time I would need Doug to sacrifice his personal needs to console me became shorter and shorter. Eventually, Doug was able to start his days without my pitiful "wailing and gnashing of teeth." However, during the day, I would still burst into unexpected and uncontrollable tears and need his comforting touch. My incredibly patient husband stopped whatever he was doing to hug and console me. Often after one of my crying episodes, we would sit and tell a fun story about Jay that would make us both laugh.

Supporting Each Other - Doug's Perspective

It's true - BJ grieved long and hard and it totally exhausted and depleted her energy. I, on the other hand, grieved in short bursts. I became overwhelmingly sad and withdrawn and usually cried for just a few minutes. After experiencing such unexpected strong emotions for me, I needed something ... anything that would focus my attention elsewhere. I often needed to escape the emotional pain and do something that took my mind off my sadness. I would go into work for a while, watch TV or read the paper. I have talked to many fathers and stepfathers who needed to grieve in this way. I don't think we were trying to avoid grieving as much as we were just trying to give ourselves a break from the deep sorrow in an attempt to manage our grief.

I believe BJ and I were both amazingly accepting and supportive of our different ways of grieving; I cried infrequently, BJ often. Supporting each other, even when we could not understand our partner's method of grieving was a tremendous help in getting us through that first year feeling connected. Our choice to do that was a conscious decision and very important to each of us.

Step Parent Issues

With that in mind, there are three areas we will concentrate on that relate to step parents after the death of a child:
1. How and why step parents feel left out
2. How a step parent and parent can help one another through the grieving process
3. How to preserve the marriage and blended family after the death of a child

Some people say that step parents are "the forgotten mourners." It was probably a step parent who said that. As we researched and considered material for this book, we found there is very limited information available to help step parents as they grieve for a deceased child and grapple with understanding the depth of a birth parent's grief.

Writing about this has helped me realize how much my "testosterone male nature" made me want to "fix" the problem. I see how that led me to become the "instant helper" in my family's journey of grief. I wanted to fix the unfixable for them instead of taking care of my own grieving needs in our time of crisis. I learned it was important for me to address my own grief and take care of my own needs, too. In our household, we passed the support baton back and forth, depending on who was suffering the most.

Personal Insight

As a step parent who has experienced the death of a stepson, I am able to share my personal insights and observations from that unique close perspective. It all started when B.J., the birth parent, and I, the step-parent-to-be, were dating.

One of our discussions during our engagement was how to handle the step parent issue. After talking it through, we made a decision that, although I was not the birth parent of Jeff and Jay, I would still have influence on them and would develop into the father figure they needed at that stage in their lives. We agreed that, even though I hadn't been able to raise them physically, I could be a big part of helping to raise them spiritually. Jeff and Jay were never referred to as "my" sons or "your stepsons" but as "our" sons. Early in our marriage we made it a priority that we were a family unit.

Length of Time and Closeness of Relationship

The closeness of the relationships with a step child can vary greatly depending on the number of years you knew your step child before he or she died and the amount of quality and quantity of time spent with the child.

Different age categories:
1. Becoming the step parent of an infant (under age 1)
2. Becoming a step parent of a pre-school child (ages 2-5)
3. Becoming the step parent of a grade school child or pre-teen (ages 6-12)
4. Becoming the step parent of a teen (ages 13-17)
5. Becoming the step parent of a young adult (age 18-21)
6. Becoming the step parent of an adult (age 22 and older)

Jeff and Jay were already young adults in college when I met them. At separate times, both Jeff and Jay came to work for me as real estate appraisal trainees. I really enjoyed those years! Working with them for eight hours a day, five days a week, I got to know them so much better than if we had only seen each other on birthdays and holidays. Later, they both became successful as top appraisers for national banks.

Jay and I shared a passion for many sports and enjoyed competing against one another in tennis. The four of us "had a ball" playing on the same co-ed softball team and, according to BJ, had limited success trying to coach her on how to play the outfield. We believed "a family that played together stayed together."

As the years passed, I felt more comfortable in my role as the head of the household, with both Jeff and Jay referring to me as "Pop". We all felt fortunate that our blended family was working smoothly.

Well ... smoothly that is, except for one area: Our fun loving Jay was quickly becoming a party animal who often consumed excess alcohol. His partying mindset led him to make poor choices with unfortunate consequences. On one trip to the desert, he borrowed Jeff's 4-wheel ATV (an all-terrain vehicle) and, under the influence of alcohol, drove it into a deep water canal in the middle of the night. Fortunately, Jay was not seriously injured, but Jeff's ATV was totaled, leading Jeff to vocalize his displeasure. BJ, Jeff, and I intervened and confronted Jay about his wild and crazy choices and tried to counsel him about his irresponsible behavior, but he didn't take this incident or his drinking seriously; he just laughed it all off.

What we didn't realize at the time was that Jay, like his birth father, was becoming more and more manic depressive (also known as bi-polar), meaning that he suffered significant mood swings, from very high and happy, to very low, depressed states. He reasoned, mistakenly, that drinking alcohol would anesthetize his depression and make him feel better. In actuality, alcohol, because it is a depressant, accelerated his downward spiral of depression.

After Jay's death, we realized his suicide must have occurred during one of his very low points. He shielded us from his increasingly depressed and melancholy side by not communicating with or visiting us during those times. We only saw the happy, gregarious, party-hearty, perpetual motion college student. What we didn't know was that Jay was actively fighting depression in a struggle for his life. Our ignorance about the silent war that was raging inside of Jay made us powerless to help him.

Supporting Each Other - Other Peoples' Perspectives

We read about a man who became a step parent after the child had died. This was a particular challenge for him because he had no history with the child. How could he grieve the loss? He made a decision to find out as much as he could about the child, not only from his spouse but from other family members, from home movies, and from reading journals and papers written by his step daughter. In that way, he was able to develop a history and could grieve to some extent with other family members.

Perhaps, most importantly, his wife found his efforts to get to know her daughter to be a great support to her. It was a beautiful act of love that helped sustain the marriage and bring them closer together as she continued to process her grief over the tragic loss of her daughter.

On the other hand, we personally know a couple where the stepfather and stepson were always at odds with each other. The new husband had become the head of the house – much to the dismay of and rejection by the teen. You might say there was "no love lost" between them. When the son died, the stepfather found it hard to relate to the birth mother's deep grief or to grieve the loss himself. It is still an area that separates the husband and wife more than ten years after the death.

We shared these two stories at a workshop with a man who had married a grieving mother five years after the death of a child he hadn't known. The couple rarely talked about the little boy. He didn't realize how important it was to learn about and talk about the deceased child. He didn't realize what a soothing balm it is for a parent to their child's name or to share the memories of their life together.

How I Felt Supported – BJ's Perspective

There are many ways a step parent can lovingly support a birth parent in his or her grief. Doug supported me in several ways by:

1. Accepting my way of grieving instead of comparing it to his.
2. Holding me whenever I cried and needed to be held.
3. Listening to me as I poured my heart out about Jay.
4. Not trying to fix or rush me through my grief.
5. Taking the lead at home in doing the chores, paying the bills, etc.
6. Fending off telephone calls and visitors who were draining my already depleted energy level.
7. Agreeing, when we ventured out in public, that we could leave if it became too difficult for either one of us to be there. (That happened on more than one occasion.)

Doug's Perspective

As I, Doug, read the things BJ listed that I did to help support her in her grief, I realize that a birth parent might support his or her spouse in almost all of the SAME WAYS. So supporting a birth parent's grief might not be a matter of doing anything differently as a step parent. However, a step parent might have to be the one sacrificing more often than vice versa, depending on the length and depth of the birth parent's grief.

Points for married couples to ponder
1. Have you felt that the death of the child put a strain on your marriage?
2. Do you feel surviving your child's death together has brought you and your marriage or family closer?
3. We can choose to make preserving the marriage a high priority. Surviving tragedy together can strengthen our unity if we look for ways to go through it together. Love is the common bond we share with each other as survivors. So whether we are birth parents or step parents, we can choose to love our spouse unconditionally through this sad and extremely challenging season in our lives.

Mother Teresa said, "In this life we cannot do great things. We can only do small things with great love."

As we continue to support each other during the years of grief, hopefully we will grow even closer together in our marriages and other family relationships, whether we are a birth parent, step parent, grandparent or relative.

Part 2

Enduring
The Healing

A butterfly lights beside us like a sunbeam,
and for a brief moment it's glory
and beauty belong to our world.
But then it flies on again
and though we wish it could have stayed,
We feel so very lucky to have seen it........

Author Unknown

4
Sharing
the Journey

Confusion

When our children die before we do, it disturbs the natural order of things. Compounding the death of a child is the loss of the future with that child - sharing their milestones – graduations, a wedding, grandchildren, birthdays, holidays, etc.

At the time of Jay's death, it seemed impossible for us to get our feet back on the ground. We questioned, "How can anyone ever heal from the deep dark pit of hopelessness?" We know it will take a lifetime to recuperate from the tragedies we don't understand. We wish there were a way for all of us to bring back all of our precious children, but there isn't. We found it cathartic, however, to write about our experiences in an effort to band together with other grieving parents so that we might help each other recover. As our recovery continued, we discovered that it is not only possible to crawl out of the pit of devastation, but to go on to achieve even greater things than we believed were possible after such a loss.

Ways We Grieve

In our grief journey, we Jensens have learned that, despite what some well-intentioned books instruct, or what some professionals who have never experienced the death of a child advise about mourning the loss of a dream or a lost pregnancy, there is no set way to grieve and that no two people will grieve the death of a child in the same way.

Unpredictable feelings and emotions bounce all-around like a crazy ball, with twists and turns and sudden drops for some people like BJ. The healing journey for her has been equivalent to riding an emotional roller coaster. And BJ says, "I don't know about you, but with my susceptibility to motion sickness, the ups and downs of roller coasters and I have never gotten along!"

Three things that have helped us are knowing that:
1. Grieving is a totally <u>unique and personal</u> experience and depends on your personality and your situation.
2. Grieving is a <u>process</u> that sometimes takes a lifetime.
3. Grieving can often follow an unpredictable two steps forward and one step back <u>pattern</u> as you move toward healing through the *stages of grief.*

The Stages of Grief

Some key points we've learned:
- There is no progressive order or length of time for each stage of grief.
- People move in and out of the different stages of grief in their own timing.
- Some stages of grief may overlap.
- We may get thrown back into some of the stages we've already worked through because of holidays, anniversaries, and other dates that trigger memories.
- We don't need to listen to others who try to tell us how we SHOULD or SHOULD NOT grieve. It's not appropriate to tell yourself or anyone else what or how they "should" feel

These are the stages of grieving we went through after our devastating losses.

A. SHOCK and DENIAL

When the doorbell rang that fateful morning, and the apologetic police detectives informed me of the tragic news as gently as they could, I immediately went into a stage that grief experts call SHOCK and DENIAL.

The shock and numbness was followed quickly by disbelief. Maybe you can relate. I said things like, "There must be a mistake," "That's not possible." "How could this be?" "I can't believe that." and "Are you SURE?" For some, shock, numbness, or denial can last days, weeks, or months.

When Doug arrived home late that afternoon he had no clue about the devastation that had overcome our family. When he walked in the house, he was told the overwhelming news. He also went into a fog-like state called shock. In a state of shock, the brain can dissolve into a jumbled haze where nothing makes sense and it is hard to remember things.

The Catching's lives were changed forever when Daisy and her husband, Dick, suffered the loss of their only child Danny who died suddenly after a heart attack. One night he was standing at the foot of his mom's bed, telling her all about his wonderful day, and the next morning he didn't wake up. Shocks like this send parents reeling.

We are just not prepared nor do we expect our children to die before we do. We expect them to outlive us, but sometimes they don't.

Triggers

Realize that sights, sounds, smells, or touch may trigger unexpected flashbacks, sweet memories, and also instant tears. The first year after Jay's death, well meaning friends inquired of BJ, "How ya doing?" It provoked an instant flood of tears since Jay always greeted her that way. If either of us caught a glimpse of someone who looked or acted like Jay it produced immediate tears.

Sometimes it seemed like we had a "bottomless barrel of tears." We are convinced that God sees and cares about every one of our tears. We remembered that God also experienced the horrendous death of a beloved child. Did knowing this lighten our grief? Not usually. Personal grief is so focused inward in this stage. SHOCK and DENIAL are experienced by our hearts, not reasoned with our minds.

The numbness we feel in this part of the process of grieving is the body's way of shielding and protecting us from the shockingly horrific reality. It allows us to survive the initial trauma.

B. ANGER and BLAME

It is excruciatingly painful whenever a parent is separated from his or her child by death. One of the first stages of the grieving process is SHOCK and DENIAL, but it can sometimes be followed quickly by another stage - ANGER and BLAME
.

Anger may be a natural emotion when we are just trying to make sense of the senseless, when life is grossly unfair or unjust. Anger occurs as a means to release the incredible emotions created by a threatening situation and can be displayed in many different ways, some appropriate and some not so appropriate.

These are three ways we experienced ANGER and BLAME – destructively; self-destructively; and constructively.

1. **Destructively**
   This can happen if we lash out physically or verbally at others or blame innocent people or things. Destruction of material things can be harmful to property and personal safety. Destruction of relationships including co-workers, friendships, family, and marriages would fall into this category.

   We knew a distraught lady who continually lashed out at her husband who was the stepfather and his son (her stepson) by saying she wished the stepson were dead instead of her son, that her son deserved to live more than her stepson did.

   Many hurtful things can be said and done in this stage and, like toothpaste once squeezed out of a tube, they can't be easily retracted or amended.

2. **Self-Destructively**
   If we blame ourselves or develop harmful personal behavior, we may be on a slippery slope of sliding into a deeper pit of darkness. Some distraught parents turn to drinking or drugs in an effort to get rid of the pain that can't be erased. They find that pain returns in full force when the effects of the alcohol or drugs wear off.

Doug watched his Uncle Bob evolve from a fun-loving, gregarious man to a bitter, sarcastic, angry person after the love of his life, Aunt Jaci, died. Uncle Bob's emotions became unbridled and uncontrolled as he focused his anger toward his self at first for being helpless to save Aunt Jaci. Then Uncle Bob turned his anger and blame toward God for allowing her death. Now, he will have nothing to do with God and will not allow family members to speak in his presence about the comfort God can give bleeding hearts. He self destructively turned his back on the One who could help him through the valley of the shadow of death.

ANGER and BLAME were self-destructive in the case of Uncle Bob, but easy for BJ to understand and relate to. She remembers being angry and turning that anger inward, too. She blamed herself for not being a better mom; she was angry because her own life continued when her son, who was in the prime of his life, was gone. She was angry at Jay for choosing a permanent solution to solve his temporary problem.

We were angry at and blamed the police officer who chased Jay when he was crying out for help and threatening to jump off the bridge. The officer's sudden aggression toward Jay caused him to make a rash decision to run and jump when he might just as easily have been talked out of it.

The intense emotions of this stage made it almost frightening to us. We didn't realize how deeply we could feel about injustice. ANGER and BLAME was a stage that we chose to pass through quickly and, unlike Doug's Uncle Bob, not live there.

3. **Constructively**

   An example is parents who are motivated to right a wrong by perhaps initiating legislation to save others from the same fate.

   Our anger over Jay's wrongful death motivated us to do something constructive. A family friend who was also a Chief of Police told us that officers have little training in stress situations like Jay's. However, the officers are taught to only *talk to*, but NEVER to be aggressive nor make a forward move toward a distraught or suicidal person. We tried talking to city officials to no avail and found we needed to bring a wrongful death lawsuit against the police department, the police officer, and the city of San Diego in order to be heard. We prayed the lawsuit would convince the city to change the way they handled life-threatening situations. We wanted them to implement a program that would provide for a properly trained mental health specialist to accompany officers whenever they answered a "distressed person" call. When the police department agreed to do that, we dropped the lawsuit, even though we had already spent nearly $20,000 to initiate it.

   It was a short time after Jay's death and the subsequent lawsuit that we read in the *San Diego Union Tribune* about a novel program implemented by the San Diego Police Department - the first of its kind in the nation. This new program called P.E.R.T. (Psychiatric Emergency Response Team) paired each of fourteen psychologists with a police officer and stationed them throughout the county. These teams respond to any calls that involve people who are mentally ill or acting oddly. The article explained that, since officers are not trained to deal with or diagnose the mentally ill, the presence of a psychologist makes the officer's job much easier. Initiated in 1996 with one team, the program has been growing steadily ever since. Currently, in San Diego County alone, there are approximately 20,000 calls per year utilizing P.E.R.T. with each team averaging three calls per shift. The article made no mention of Jay, however.

A few years later, BJ was a speaker at a women's conference. During her talk, she mentioned the tragic wrongful death of our son and our subsequent lawsuit. At the end of the talk, a tearful young lady approached BJ and shared an amazing story. She conveyed to BJ that she was getting married that summer to a young man who had also stood on the Coronado Bridge the previous year threatening to jump.

She continued her amazing story by saying that when the police department received the emergency call about a "potential jumper" on the Coronado Bridge, police were immediately dispatched to the scene along WITH a mental health specialist. The professional talked to the troubled man and offered him help and hope, convincing him NOT to jump but to seek psychiatric help instead. After a series of counseling sessions, her fiancé had completely turned his life around. With professional help, he had solved the problems that had once seemed insurmountable.

We thanked God that we were able to see that a good program had been finally put in place and was working to save other families from the horrendous grief we had gone through.

Other Constructive Outlets

Shortly after Jay's death, BJ was hired as the Drama Director and Sketch Writer at our church. She expressed difficult-to-deal-with emotions by pouring her heart out on paper and writing poignant sketches. Because writing and journaling help us to process many of our deepest thoughts and feelings, it can be a good outlet for those who grieve.

BJ wrote a monologue portraying a lady dealing with feelings of ANGER and BLAME. The lady in the sketch had returned to work after the death of her child and all of her co-workers assumed that, because she was back to work, that everything was "back to normal." What most people don't realize is that things never get "back to normal" after the death of a child, that we have to take an active role in slowly creating our new "normal." The sketch was eye-opening to many, and a stress reliever for BJ.

Anger Masks Underlying Pain

Sometimes we mask our anguish with displays of ANGER or BLAME, but underneath hides unresolved hurt and pain. Talking about that pain and expressing it through writing are both highly recommended and helpful outlets.

Linda Stirling found herself stuck in rush hour traffic. It was months after the shocking death of her eldest son in a plane crash. With tears flowing, she pounded on the steering wheel, angry at her son for dying. "How could you have done this? You were such a good pilot!"

It seemed like his voice came from the radio and spoke directly to her heart, "Mom, don't be mad at me. I didn't mean to." Her heart melted. The pent-up anger was released as she answered back, "I know you didn't mean to. I'm not mad at you anymore. Really." The destructive weight of her poisonous anger dissipated. The experience freed her from the prison of anger that had crippled her healing.

During this stage of our healing, the strong negative emotions scared us enough to choose NOT to reside in that valley. We reached out for help verbally and in writing because we realized that, no matter how intense our feelings became, they wouldn't bring back our beloved son. We are each grateful that we had the help of a loving spouse, who was also an encouraging friend, to help us move _through_ the stage of ANGER and BLAME.

A single parent going through grief can seek out a family member or special friend to help them through the tough times. We all need a special friend who can stand by and protect us as we grieve. If you don't already have a special someone "to hold that umbrella for you in your storm," look for the one who wants to be there for you at your nearest meeting of people who have experienced a similar loss. He or she may be at a COMPASSIONATE FRIENDS meeting, or a meeting of the UMBRELLA MINISTRIES, a S.I.D.S. (Sudden Infant Death Syndrome) support group, or an S.O.S.L. (Survivors of Suicide) group. Everyone at these specially focused groups can understandably empathize with you and help you in the healing journey.

Other Constructive Examples

We've looked at some of the ways ANGER and BLAME can be *destructive* to those around us, *self-destructive* and *constructive.* Anger gave us the energy to do something about an injustice. Anger can right a wrong. Trying to right the wrong will not bring our child back, but it may help other families avoid a similar devastating experience.

In 1980, Candy Lightner was outraged when her daughter Cari was struck and killed by a repeat drunk-driving offender. She founded MADD (Mothers Against Drunk Driving), an organization that is still successfully campaigning against drunk driving thirty years later.

In 1996, public outrage over the abduction and murder of 9-year-old Amber Hagerman of Arlington, Texas ignited the implementation of a new warning system called Amber Alert. Using this system allows law enforcement and the public to instantly know when a child has been abducted or is missing. It quickly became a national movement with subsequent implementation of Amber Alert Programs in every state. As of January 7, 2010, the Amber Alert Program was directly responsible for the safe recovery of 495 children.

The murder of seven-year-old Megan Kanka at the hands of a previously-convicted sex offender who, with four other sex offenders, lived across the street, led to the passage of Megan's Law. This law requires the registration of sex offenders in a database tracked by the state. It also requires community notification and posting of the sex offender's living addresses.

Peer counseling and citizen-driven legislation are both forms of engagement that yield unmistakable and positive results. Brent and Kelly King campaigned until Chelsea's Law was signed by Governor Schwarzenegger in California in 2010 because of the rape and murder of their vivacious, beautiful high school student Chelsea by a repeat child molester. This law calls for life imprisonment without the possibility of parole for convicted child molesters.

Now, the Kings have chosen to devote the rest of their lives to championing this "one-strike" law for sex offenders by introducing Chelsea's Law in the other forty-nine states. Although working for Chelsea's Law continually puts the Kings in a place that reminds them of her death, they have chosen to remember her life in a positive way by establishing the Chelsea's Light Foundation which creates opportunities for children to realize their dreams through the Sunflower Scholarship Fund and Chelsea's Light Peer Corps in high schools.

Mo Dubois, father of freshman Amber, who was missing for more than a year and found buried in a shallow grave, turned his rage into action when he founded More Kids, Inc., an organization that seeks to assist the families of missing children and to help prevent the abduction of and sexual violence against children.

Although anger is inevitable, we have the ability to choose whether we will allow it to become destructive to others, self-destructive, or a powerfully motivating constructive force. The choice is ours. As bereaved parent Denise Howard Pederson says, "Grief and loss allows ordinary people to do EXTRAORDINARY things."

C. BARGAINING and GUILT

A distinctly different stage in our grief journey is BARGAINING and GUILT.

Did you ever find yourself trying to promise or bargain with the doctors, with God, or with anyone who would listen? "Please let him or her live … I'll do ANYTHING!" or "Take me instead … just don't take her." "Let my child live … and I'll…. (You can fill in the blank.)"

I, Doug, finally realized I personally needed to stop the "If only" record playing over and over in my head, the one that says, "If only I had been there." or "If only I had called Jay that morning." "If only he had let me know." I was stuck in this repetitive cycle for at least two years. I now believe it probably stemmed from my feelings of helplessness and hopelessness surrounding Jay's death. After all, I am a guy. Guys like to fix things. I couldn't fix the unfixable. I felt guilty. Guilt is painful and hard to deal with.

Did you ever have thoughts that your child's death was your fault? That you didn't do everything you could have, should have, or ought to have done to prevent their death?

Here is an excerpt from "The What If? Trap" - an article written by Clara Hinton in 2002:

> *Probably the longest-lasting, most tormenting emotion of all following the death of a child is that of guilt. That unanswerable question comes to the forefront of our thoughts and just won't leave. What if? What if I had not left the pills sitting on the kitchen table? What if I had not left the keys in the unlocked car? What if I had stayed close to the pool and kept my eyes on him? What if I had not left the gun cabinet unlocked?*

There is a knife-sharp pain sent through the heart of a parent time and time again when guilt penetrates all thoughts. Guilt places a heavy burden that just seems to paralyze all thoughts from ever moving beyond that one unanswerable question -"What if? "What if I had only done or said things just a bit differently? Maybe then I'd still have my precious child."

Forgiveness

Moving beyond guilt is a necessary step in the journey of healing from the loss of a child. This particular part of grief can be the most difficult pain of all to overcome. In order to be free of guilt, it is necessary to ask for forgiveness of God, of your child, of oneself and if appropriate of others who are suffering the loss of your child.

God and your child will always forgive you because they love you and do not want you to continue to suffer guilt and sadness. They want you to lead a life of purpose with joy.

Others, including a spouse or close relative, may not be willing to forgive right away, perhaps never. But asking for forgiveness can free you of the burden of quilt, even if others choose not to let go of their grief and hopelessness.

Perhaps the most difficult test is forgiving your self. When we refuse to forgive, we are held captive like a convicted criminal. Not forgiving sentences a person to a horrible life in a prison of our own making – one where we barely exist. It is difficult but a necessary step in order to move toward the point of healing. Sometimes forgiving takes the help of a trained professional or counselor. Are you willing to forgive yourself or do you want to stay captive on a downward-spiraling path of self-loathing?

Many children's deaths are accidental, and a life can end in only seconds. No parent can completely foolproof a child's life. The tragic truth is that fatal accidents can and do happen every hour. When this happens, it is very common for a parent to fall into the self-damaging cycle of the "what if" or guilt trap. Moving through the guilt of this unanswerable question often causes endless tears. Discussing the guilt has helped many parents to move beyond the "what if" trap. Tell those closest to you why you feel guilty, and ask for help. Although you may occasionally get a careless, hurtful response, family and friends will respond most often with compassion. Recognizing and admitting your feelings of guilt is a critical first step.

Put down on paper how you feel. Don't leave anything out. Plan some sort of "letting go" ritual as a means of moving past your guilt. You might read aloud all of your guilty feelings to your spouse or to two or three close friends and then crumble the paper and toss it into a fire with all of your guilt. As you watch the paper burn, you may begin to feel your heavy burden lighten.

Finally, you must realize that without forgiving yourself, you will never be able to move forward. You must make a determined effort to not allow yourself to ask the "what if" question. It is a futile question with no answer, and only adds to your grief.

By taking very precise steps to rid yourself of guilt, you will lift a heavy burden and finally be able to move forward in your journey of grief. Once you can move beyond the "what if" trap, you will know that you have successfully gotten rid of the gnawing questions that never really have any answers. Healing is about to begin!

We really need to stop playing the "coulda, shoulda, woulda" games in our minds. They aren't productive and won't reverse the irreversible past. We need to make the decision to stop "shoulding" all over ourselves. When a child dies, no amount of bargaining or guilt will bring him or her back. The BARGAINING and GUILT stage is another one we need to consciously choose to pass through quickly and not take up residency.

D. DEPRESSION and HOPELESSNESS

This stage of grief, DEPRESSION and HOPELESSNESS, might come and go throughout our journey toward healing. Sometimes, the closer the attachment to the one who has died, the deeper and longer the depression or hopelessness may be.

Although everyone goes through depression before they can heal from a major loss, if not checked, a downward spiral of misery and despair can develop. If you feel that you or a loved one are hopelessly depressed or slipping away from reality because of your tremendous loss, it is advisable to seek professional evaluation and help.

BJ was seriously depressed for over a year after Jay died. She continued to suffer through the motions of living, but had lost interest in most aspects of life. There were times when she just wanted to give up. Getting to sleep was difficult. Even if she were able to get some sleep, she would be awakened in the middle of the night by the sounds of her own sobbing. This happened every night for months. It was too difficult to accept that Jay was gone, in a physical sense, for the rest of our lives. Most people don't see the behind the scenes of a grieving family. It's not a pretty sight or an easy time.

While going *through* this part of grief, life may seem point-less. That's understandable. We've just lost a huge part of our lives. It may take a longer time to work through the stage of depression than the other stages of grief. We can give ourselves all the time we need. However, if depression is adversely affecting us to the point where we are about to lose our job, our house, or our family, or if we're planning self-destructive behavior, then we need to seek professional help immediately.

With depression comes the tendency toward isolation. It is the "wounded animal instinct" to want to crawl into a cave to die solitarily. But as humans, we need to limit our isola-tion in order to protect ourselves from succumbing to the risk of unchecked depression that leads to despair and hope-lessness. Once again, it is our recommendation to reach out to others to find comfort, even when true comfort does not seem possible.

Sometimes pride, embarrassment, apathy, or finances keep us from doing what is necessary to "jump start" our own recovery. When I prayed about what God would have me do in this desolate state, I was led to write a personal postcard each day to give encouragement to someone else. In reach-ing out to others, I slowly felt my own fog lift.

Experts assure us that there is a light at the end of the tunnel of depression.. But for someone suffering the death of a child, that tunnel can seem extremely dark and long or deep. It may be difficult to see any way out because our eyes are clouded with overwhelming sadness and tears. That's when we need to reach out for a "hand up."

E. ACCEPTANCE and HOPE

We'll write more on this subject in Chapter 9, but we wanted to address it here briefly because it is one of the most important stages of the grieving process. Without ACCEPTANCE and HOPE, our lives will seem empty, meaningless, and unfocused.

Hope is the final and desired destination in the stages of grief -- the light at the end of the long dark tunnel. We don't arrive at hope without persevering through all the other painful stages of grief. We don't arrive at hope without accepting all that grief encompasses – the death of our beloved child, the unanswered questions, the lost dreams, forgiveness of ourselves and others, and finally acceptance that life goes on and that we are a valuable part of the future for our family, friends, and community. However, in order to arrive at this destination, we need to survive the first traumatic year.

**5
Surviving
the First Year**

Dark Days

When our adult son Jay chose a permanent solution to solve his temporary challenges by jumping off of the Coronado Bridge in San Diego in 1995, our family was catapulted into the darkest days of our lives. We entered into a time of grieving that was unexpected, lonely, and extremely painful. His bewildering tragic death sent us into a tailspin of personal depression, hopelessness, and soul searching. Stunned and incapacitated, we both realized that it would be a monumental challenge to survive such an overwhelming and devastating blow, let alone to find meaning in life. But we did survive.

We can say from our experiences, after the death of a beloved child, the intensity of the pain you may be experiencing today can ease up ever so gradually with the passing of time. The amount of time for the extreme pain to subside is different for everyone, and it may be a life-long process of recovery. But be assured that your life, like ours, can go on to have new meaning and significance.

To those of you who have experienced the death of your precious child in the past year - your grieving is still fresh, raw, and sometimes excruciating. You may find it hard to believe you will ever recover or heal from such a horrendous loss. Those who have walked through this experience before you would tell you, in their wisdom, that some days will be better than others; some days you will want to stay in bed and cover up your head, and some days you may feel like you're going backwards. We pray that there will be better days ahead for you.

There is no healthy way to shorten the grieving process, to make it go away, or to pretend it doesn't exist. The deeper we love, the deeper the wound that will have to heal. Just as a broken bone may take a long time to heal physically, a broken heart may take a lifetime to mend both psychologically and emotionally. There is no "set" amount of time for mourning. Some people adjust to their new "reality" in months. Others take years. For those of us experiencing the death of a loved child, it may take longer. The recommended length of time you can expect is whatever you personally need.

- Will a broken heart ever mend?   YES
- Does healing mean that we are forgetting our loved one?   NO
- Will he or she always have a place in our heart? ABSOLUTELY
- Does a lesser intensity of grief mean that we love them any less?   ABSOLUTELY NOT

As the reality of our son's death sank in during those first excruciating months of grief, life felt like a murky existence. Later, we realized it would be beneficial for us to learn what other parents did to deal with the continual aching and seemingly unbearable pain of losing a child or children. We began a quest, gathering information about what other bereaved parents found helpful in surviving that first year - when hope seemed lost and it was extremely difficult to go on. Of course, what may be helpful to one person might send the next person over the edge. Our advice is to be selective in choosing what is right for you in your healing, and not to let anyone tell you what you should or should not do.

We'll concentrate on ideas that encouraged healing in four areas of our total being – emotional, physical, mental, and spiritual.

A. Emotional Healing

It was not helpful to suppress, avoid, or postpone grief's expression. Bottling up our feelings and emotions to spare others the intensity was not advisable. We learned that one of the most effective ways to help our emotional healing was to allow ourselves to feel the pain and to talk about it regularly - as often as we could and for as long as we needed to. It was important to release these feelings. When we didn't express them in this appropriate way, they came out eventually - sometimes at inappropriate times and in inappropriate explosions.

One of the worst things about bottling up emotions is that they implode – go inward and break down the immune system making us vulnerable to illness.

We learned to give ourselves permission to cry - as much and as often as we needed. We dismissed voices from our past that said, "Don't' cry!" or "Keep a stiff upper lip." We all have hidden voices with messages similar to these: "Only babies cry"; "Real men don't cry"; "Pull yourself up by your bootstraps"; "Buckle up"; "Get a hold of yourself." Actually, physiologically, it is quite healthy to cry. Tears are not only cleansing, but therapeutic, releasing endorphins, natural opiates, in the body. Endorphins in our tears help us feel better so that we can heal. Tears are also a release valve for the pressure that builds up in the heart. Mourners can expect their tears to run as deep as their love for their children.

Grief impacts individuals and marriages in strong emotional ways. Some hurting couples acknowledge their child's "death day" annually. Others reveal the difficult emotions when finally deciding to pack away their child's clothing, toys, and memorabilia. One father took years before he could bring himself to repaint his son's bedroom, where the boy's fingerprints were still visible on parts of the wall, and where his son had secretly scribbled his girlfriend's phone number. Some couples find it helpful to discuss the painful disappointment from close family and friends who, because they were uncertain about how to deal with the loss, said nothing at all, or something deeply hurtful.

BJ's Emotions

I cried more tears that first year after Jay died then I had cried in my whole life. On some nights, I quietly cried myself to sleep. On other nights, I was not able to get to sleep because of uncontrollable sobbing. Some nights I succumbed to sleep out of pure exhaustion after crying what seemed like a river of tears. Every night for months, I would be startled awake in the middle of the night with the sound of my own deep wailing that could last for hours.

I am thankful my patient and understanding husband would simply hold me until the weeping subsided. I know it wasn't easy for him to listen as my heart broke over and over, but I am so grateful he allowed me to grieve in the way that came naturally for me.

Grieving is exhausting. Unless we take care of ourselves emotionally, the grieving that depletes our energy level will leave little concern for anything else. If you feel like you are "falling to pieces" it is good to share your feelings with supportive loved ones. If you are not surrounded by friends or family who are supportive and who encourage your expression of grief, consider doing an Internet search for and attending a support group in your hometown. Some excellent support is available through local chapters of COMPASSIONATE FRIENDS, UMBRELLA MINISTRIES, S.O.S.L., or GRIEFSHARE. If these groups have not yet started in your city, there may be other support groups at your church, temple, or synagogue. At these meetings, <u>everyone</u> will comprehend and empathize with what you are going through.

Things We Learned

Some of the things we learned that helped us heal emotionally:
1. <u>Feeling</u> the pain was a necessary part of grieving.
2. <u>Discussing</u> grief openly and honestly was best.
3. <u>Being</u> patient with oneself and others who were grieving helped.
4. <u>Accepting</u> stronger feelings that ebbed and flowed as part of the normal grieving experience was important.
5. <u>Knowing</u> the intensity of the pain would subside.
6. <u>Comparing</u> personal healing to someone else's healing was counterproductive.
7. <u>Going</u> through the mourning process at one's own personal pace was best.

8. Suppressing grief/feelings/emotions to spare other people from being uncomfortable was not helpful for sanity's sake.

9. Realizing that there would be bad days. The course of grief followed no predictable pattern. At some points in the second year, the pain was worse than the first. After experiencing a good day or two, we were sometimes lulled into thinking the worst was over, or that we were past the deep pain. When a bad day came along, it made us feel like we had done something wrong to put ourselves back at the starting line. Unfortunately, the ups, downs, and setbacks were all part of the process

10. Trusting that we would survive, even though we truly doubted it.

Different Ways to Grieve

Because we are all unique individuals, each of us will work through grief in our own way, in our own time, and at our own pace. Some of us have to take it one day at a time, some, one hour at a time, and others, moment by moment.

Our unique personalities coupled with the relationship we had with our child and the manner in which he or she died, will dictate the length and depth of our own journey.

We discovered early on that marriage partners, as well as siblings, handle strong feelings and emotions quite differently. There are five ways we have identified:

1. Some People Choose To Grieve Privately. Regardless of whether they were taught to do it that way in their family of origin or because they don't want to burden others, isolation is not the healthiest choice for a griever. Segregating oneself can lead to a downward spiral of depression with the risk of ending up all alone at the bottom of a deep dark hole. It is good to reach out to others to share the burden of grief.

2. Some May Clam Up And Choose Never To Talk About It. Our oldest son, Jeff fell into this category. He closed that chapter of his life with his best friend and brother as though a friend had left in the heat of an argument, never to be spoken of again. In some ways, it was easy to understand his choice at the time because it seemed less painful. However, death is a fact that will not go away and we will be called to deal with the reality of it sooner or later.

We are reminded of two other people who chose this approach. One chose to divorce his wife and the past so he wouldn't have to face the hurt any longer. One decided to blame God and never talk to Him again. Both men thought they had unburdened themselves of the death of a loved one. They chose not to face or deal with the excruciating pain. Both have become hardened by their choices.

3. Some People Are <u>Natural "Fixers"</u> They want to fix it, make it go away, or make it all better. The impossibility of trying to "fix" a child's death ultimately leads to frustration, as it did with my sweet wonderful Doug, the fixer, trying to fix the unfixable.

4. Some <u>Run From Displays Of Raw Emotions</u> because they don't know how to handle or deal with such powerful feelings. Doug chose this method in the beginning of our marriage whenever I, BJ, would cry. But once Doug realized that he wouldn't be able to run away from emotions during our hoped-for fifty plus years of marriage, he chose to change his perspective. He learned to speak the language of feelings and to deal with the tears at the time they flowed. We are both grateful he made that decision before Jay's death.

5. Some <u>Face The Emotions</u> and work through them. We are grateful that we eventually decided to face the raw emotions together and help each other through the tough days. If you have other children at home, they will need to talk about and deal with their emotions and grieving, too. It's good to ask individual family members what helps and what doesn't help them, and then respect those wishes.

Doug and I agreed that whenever we were both crying, we'd cry on each other's shoulder. If I were the one experiencing the explosive emotions, I asked Doug to simply hold me- sometimes for hours. We always lent an ear to the other when needing to talk through feelings. When Doug was the one experiencing a tough time, he would ask for his head, neck, or back to be rubbed to reduce the stress and tightness he felt. We tried our best to support and comfort each other through the valley. We consciously allowed each other to feel the emotions and talk through the emotions we were experiencing.

Physical Healing

We heard people admit many different things at support meetings we attended.

"I expected my emotions would betray me, but I didn't anticipate how my body would betray me when I was the most vulnerable."

Digestive disturbances, elevated blood pressure, increased heart rate, shallow or fast breathing, headaches, muscle pains, and trouble concentrating are just a few of the physical ailments we might experience after the death of a loved one.

"Sometimes I feel like an elephant is sitting on my chest."

"My hands are freezing cold, like they're in a bucket of ice water. I've never had this kind of sensation before."

"I catch myself sighing or hyperventilating a lot."

"My body feels so weak and tired that I physically collapse half way through the day."

We were comforted in knowing the way we were feeling was not just "all in our head." Through the experience of Jay's death, we learned that a mother could be affected and suffer the pain of this shocking tragedy in every part of her **physical** being. Children are a part of us and a piece of our soul that has been ripped away.

Some people experience symptoms such as aches and pains because grief often manifests itself physically. Grieving will break down the immune system making it easier to become physically ill. Don't dismiss persistent physical ailments or symptoms -- ask your doctor's advice. Strong daily vitamins might be a good preventative measure to boost your immune system.

How Can I Take Care of Me When I Don't Have The Energy?

It is really important to take care of ourselves physically because our bodies are the only earthly vehicles we'll ever have. We need them now and will need them to function well in the future.

1. **Establish A Routine As Soon As Possible.** Humans thrive on orderliness and routine. The death of a loved one disturbs this orderliness in the most devastating manner possible.

    Good grooming may be an extreme effort in the first year, but physical appearance is a critical step toward restoring a sense of well-being and balance. It may take great effort to shower and shave when you don't feel like it. But even when we didn't feel like brushing our teeth or getting dressed, we did it anyway. It became okay to try to act okay until we became okay.

    Re-establishing routine by returning to the work force is a major and necessary step. Although the right time will be different for everyone, we recommend getting back to work as soon as you are capable. For many bereaved, it is an economic necessity to return to work soon after the funeral is over. Some find solace in their work while some postpone returning to work fearing the additional job-related stress. However, most employers are compassionate and sympathetic. Some have firsthand knowledge of loss and grief and extend encouragement and understanding.

    The week after Jay's Memorial Service I, BJ, was sched-uled to act in a drama with my friends Peggy and Phil. The drama was about a lady sitting in the "heavenly waiting room" waiting to be called into heaven. Realizing it was an extremely sensitive subject for me, my understanding boss, Pastor Jeanette, told me she was willing to cancel the drama. After praying about it, I told her I wanted to go ahead with the drama because I needed something constructive to keep my mind occupied. Everyone has different needs and capabilities.

Some bosses have a very unrealistic opinion of how long it takes to "get over" a family member's death and may NOT be as tolerant of grieving in the office, with the worker's preoccupation, or with trips to the bathroom to dry tears.

It is advisable to discuss your limits and concerns with your employer, and perhaps arrive   at a compromise where you are allowed to work a few hours a day in the beginning.

2. **Get Plenty Of Rest.** Sleep is therapeutic and healing. Although individuals have different needs, seven to nine hours minimum is recommended for most. Avoiding stimulants in the evening helps prepare the body for restful sleep. Caffeinated foods, including chocolate and most cola drinks, are sleep robbers. Natural sleep aids like melatonin can be helpful. However, before supplementing or self-medicating, you should discuss any sleep problems with your personal physician and agree on what would work best for you.

3. **Get Regular Exercise.** The important thing is to not overdo it. Find out what exercise is agreeable to your body. Walking briskly in the fresh air, swimming, and biking can all help release endorphins and make you feel better. Although it takes self-discipline, daily exercise is nature's best anti-depressant and sleep enhancer.

Find out what time of the day is best for you. Exercising too late in the afternoon or evening may be a stimulator that also could rob you of sleep. However, some bodies respond to late exercise by sleeping more soundly. Find out what your body prefers.

At the time of Jay's death, we had two big dogs that depended on us to get out and walk them twice a day. Looking after their needs, although it seemed like a disruptive chore, was actually a blessing because it got us up and moving, and thinking about something beyond our sorrow.

4. **Eat Healthy Foods Regularly.** Some grievers might find it hard to even eat at all. Don't allow your self to get too hungry or to go without meals. Your body needs fuel to heal. On the other hand, try not to overeat. Some grievers experience a gnawing, empty feeling that we mistake as hunger and seek to fill with food.

After Jay's death, BJ gained fifteen pounds. She now realizes that the constant, uneasy rolling feeling in her stomach was not hunger for food but rather an unsettling hunger to   have Jay back. After she became wise to what was happening, she sought help to get back on the healthy weight track.

5. **Do Not Overdo Anything.** This includes sleeping, exercising, eating, or indulging in any other addictive substances. Sometimes we turn to things that are not healthy for us. Even though it is tempting to numb the pain of grief with a drink and try to avoid feeling the acute grief by popping a pill, we need to avoid the possible increase of ALL addictive substances including alcohol, drugs, tobacco, self-medication, prescription drugs, and believe it or not - sugar. What is addictive to one person may be fine for another. If you think you may be eating too much of something, you probably are. If you suspect something may be an addiction, it probably is.

Addictions may help us feel a bit better for a little while, but they spike you up   momentarily and then drop your mood level down lower than where you started. Addictive substances actually magnify an already depressed state of mind. Alcohol, drugs, tobacco, self-medication, prescription drugs and sugar *do not* contribute to our well being. They *do* mask feelings, lower inhibitions and deprive us of self-discipline. The reality of our unwanted situation will have to be faced and experienced sooner or later. Sooner and clear-headed is better!

Mental Healing

Alison Lighthall, RN, MSN and Psychiatric Nurse Consultant says, "Severe psychological trauma is a special kind of broken-heartedness. It takes up residency in you, sometimes making itself known in cruel ways and other times taking a quiet nap from which it can be quickly and easily aroused.

It is a permanent condition that, on some rare and lucky occasions, eases with time or goes blessedly into dormancy but never actually ends."

How deeply do you think your mental state was affected by the death of your child? Did you sometimes feel like you were going crazy? I (BJ) did! I experienced lapses of memory, complete blank-outs, and found it very difficult, if not impossible, to focus at times. My mental state was foggy and, even worse, most of the time, I didn't even care!

The only time I did care was when others were counting on me. One time I was leading our signing choir in a church service and my mind went completely blank. I was out in front of the group and the choir was following my lead, but I had no idea what to sign next in the song. Everyone was counting on me to show them what to do, and I just stood there blank. There will be days like that. Minds can shut down when they are on overload during grief. It is all part of the process of healing.

Knowing what to expect, knowing that others have been through it and survived, and knowing that mental lapses are a temporary situation may help you endure the grieving process, as it did for us.

Escaping the Pain - BJ's Perspective

My mental state was not very good the first six months. Suicidal thoughts came often and were scary for me. When Jay died, I was overwhelmed by the intensity of the sorrow and wanted to escape the pain. We may believe we cannot endure such intensity. For a time, we may not wish to.

It is normal to want to get away from the constant mental anguish of the death of a beloved child and normal to think of ending one's own life to escape the pain. But there is a considerable difference between having suicidal thoughts and acting upon them. If you are obsessed with thoughts of putting an end to your misery, if you are beginning to seriously consider a plan for ending your life, or you believe you don't deserve to live due to some circumstance surrounding your loved one's death, you really need to seek the help of a mental health professional without delay. Don't compound the loss and magnify the grief of others by resolving your own grief in this manner.

Healthy Escapes

1. **Journaling.** Writing is a great way to allow thoughts, feelings and emotions to spill onto paper and not people. We wrote stories - lots of stories! Some were published, some were not. It didn't matter. The point was that writing itself was therapeutic. Some parents write letters to their child who has died as a way to feel connected to him or her.

2. **Postponing Major Decisions** whenever possible. They can wait until you are more capable of making a good decision. Don't try to move, change jobs, throw things away, or make a big purchase. We heard about parents who regretted some of their rash decisions the first year of rebuilding their lives after the death of a child.

3. **Occupying The Mind** – Earlier, we stated that it is healthy to work through grief and not avoid it. However, just as your body would break down if you worked out at the gym sixteen hours a day, your mind also needs breaks. Try working picture puzzles, Sudoku puzzles, tackling word games, or reading to keep the mind occupied. We read books about grieving to see if we were actually going crazy. It was a relief to read the writings of others in a similar situation that said we weren't. Compassionate Friends has a Facebook page with interesting new comments and questions each day.

4. **Doing Something Pleasurable** – We recommend doing something you find enjoyable to relieve the mind from constantly dwelling on your loved one. You might need to schedule favorite activities to help you get through the days. Reading works for some. Going to the movies or going out to eat with close friends works for others. Watch or participate in sporting events can pass the time. Just getting out of the house for awhile is therapeutic for some people.

5. **Introducing Pleasant Changes** into your life. You might try something new like we did – gardening. Doug started growing tomatoes; BJ planted flowers. Maybe you have a cuddly pet that you could take to a hospital to offer pet therapy to sick children. Have you ever tried scrapbooking? Many people organize an album that honors the life of their son or daughter. I found that helpful. Now I have a "Jay" album I can visit whenever I need.

Beth took up knitting to occupy her mind and hands. If you are a real seamstress, like our talented friend Debbie, maybe your local community theater would be grateful for a volunteer seamstress. Even though I do not sew, I went so far as to try my hand at quilting and made a special love quilt from Jay's dressy work shirts. Now I can cuddle in "Jay's Quilt" when I'm feeling lonely for his bear hugs.

Whatever it is, finding a project that works for you and that requires time and thought really does help to divert the mind.

6. **Writing Poetry.** Some people find this helpful.

A DOZEN ROSES
By Alan Pedersen

If I had a dozen roses, I know just what I'd do
I'd give each one a name that reminded me of you.
The first rose I'd call **SUNSHINE**,
because you brighten every day,
The second would be **BEAUTY**,
the kind that never goes away.
The third rose would be **PRICELESS**,
like those hugs you gave to me,
I'd name the fourth rose **SILLY**,
oh how funny you could be.
Rose five of course is **PATIENCE**,
something you have helped me find

The sixth rose would be **MEMORIES,**
the gift you left behind.
The seventh and the eighth rose
would for sure be **FAITH** and **GRACE,**
Nine would be **UNIQUE**
because no one can take your place.
The tenth rose well that's easy,
I'd simply name it **LOVE,**
Eleven would be **ANGEL**
- I know you're watching from above.
I'd think about that twelfth rose,
and I'd really take my time
After all these roses are for you,
my Valentine
I'm sending them to heaven
in every color that I know
So rose twelve will be **FOREVER,**
that's how long I'll love you so.

7. **Making a Conscious Decision** to be an active participant in your own healing. If you believe you will be better, you will get better. Learned optimism was defined by Martin Seligman and published in his 1990 book, *Learned Optimism*. Seligman invites pessimists to learn to be optimists by thinking about their reactions to adversity in a new way. The resulting optimism, one that grew out of pessimism, is a learned optimism. The mind is a powerful tool in your recovery. Although it may be easier to slip into a pessimistic, depressed state

after the death of a loved one, optimistically condition-
ing your mind that this is a *temporary* emotional state
will be instrumental in feeling better.

Spiritual Healing

The French philosopher Pierre Teilhard de Chardin (1881-
1955) said, "We are not human beings having a spiritual experience. We are spiritual beings having a human experience."

This insightful and poignant poem was written by Dana
Gensler:

> *Who could have known the exquisite difference*
> *Your brief life would make upon mine?*
> *Who could have known a tiny baby*
> *Would show me the beauty of a sunrise,*
> *Or the wonder of a rainbow,*
> *Or the pain of a tear?*
> *Who could have known an innocent child*
> *Would take away my fear of death*
> *And point me in the direction of heaven?*
> *Who would have known that you would succeed*
> *Where so many others have failed?*

For some, the death of a loved one leads them to embrace a
belief for the first time.

The death of a loved one causes some believers to question their faith.

For others, faith is a lifeline to hold onto – a spiritual buoy when your dreams have capsized.

If you are a person of faith, maintain that faith by doing the things that were important to you before the death of your loved one. Did you attend worship services at a church, synagogue, or a temple? We suggest working toward returning to the custom of attending worship services as often as you can, as your grief allows. Although crying forced BJ to leave the worship service on several occasions, we kept going back until we were able to stay the whole time.

If you haven't been attending any type of worship service, you may want to start -- like Jay's brother Jeff, and Jay's best friend Brian. They found it to be a comfort to them during an uncomfortable season of mourning when they were searching for answers.

Did you read the Bible or other spiritual readings to strengthen your faith before the death occurred? Then you should continue to do that which gave you comfort before. Did you pray? Then you should continue to pray - certainly not FOR your circumstances, but IN your circumstances. God can give a comfort and peace that passes all understanding in the midst of trials when we ask Him for that in our prayers.

It's advisable to stay connected to your support systems, such as covenant groups, social groups, Bible studies, and with spiritual leaders, as your energy level allows.

Anger at God

Motherhood arrived early and changed her life. Mandy was only seventeen years old when her beautiful baby Angelica was born, and handsome little Christian followed two years later. Soon after, the nightmare began.

Mandy's husband became increasingly abusive. His inappropriate outbursts of anger spilled over to Angelica and Christian. The day Mandy caught him shaking and yelling at their innocent five-month-old to shut him up was the day her protective mother bear instinct took over and Mandy whisked the children off to her hometown for safety. After the divorce, Mandy found that being a single mom was a financial struggle and emotionally draining. Her helpful fifteen-year-old brother moved in to babysit the toddlers while Mandy was at work.

"You need to get home immediately," screamed her brother into the phone one day. "Angelica is unconscious."

Mandy raced home and, as soon as she walked in, she could see that Angelica's face was purple, her lips were blue, and she was struggling for every breath. Mandy panicked. She rushed Angelica to the hospital. The doctors informed the police.

Mandy's brother admitted to the police that he had kicked Angelica in the back and she had flown across the room, hitting her head against the wall. Angel's skull was crushed and her brain was hemorrhaging- a trauma too severe for her to survive.

Before doctors pronounced Angelica dead, they allowed Mandy to hold her to say goodbye. She hugged her unresponsive precious bundle and told her how sorry she was for allowing this to happen to her and for not being there for her. Mandy's guilt consumed her like a tsunami swallows up everything in its path.

Mandy's younger brother was charged with manslaughter and sentenced to seven years in prison. He served his time and has since been released to return home. Sweet little Angelica will never return home.

A little over three years later, the mother of Mandy's new boyfriend was watching Christian. When Mandy asked where Christian was, her boyfriend's mom said she thought he was outside riding his bike. Mandy couldn't understand why this woman had left her three-year-old unattended. Mandy rushed outside to look for him and couldn't see him. She called and called to Christian to no avail. The frantic suffocating feeling she had experienced previously with Angelica returned.

Her family, neighbors, police, and helicopters were called in to assist in the search. Did Christian wander off? Was he kidnapped? Was he hurt and unable to get back home? The police eventually dispatched a dive team to the irrigation canal across the road. They recovered the drowned body of little Christian. He did return home - in a tiny body bag.

Words couldn't describe the anger that welled up in Mandy. She didn't know who to blame for the tragedies. She said the devil told her it was all God's fault, that He hadn't protected her children. Since she didn't want to blame herself, her brother, or her boyfriend's mother, Mandy directed her anger toward God. The pain was indescribable and incomprehensible to senselessly lose two children in three years. She cursed God. She numbed out. She had to bury her second precious baby.

Mandy's hard heart turned away from God for ten years. She has since returned to His comforting, loving arms and has become an inspirational witness to God's goodness - in spite of her tragedies. After the horrendous losses of both of her children, Mandy recently said to me, "The more I look back now, the more I realize that, instead of dealing with my issues and my hurt, I ran from them. I ran as fast as I could away from God, the only thing in this life that could ease my pain. I blamed Him. I mean, how could I trust Him? My soul and my spirit were broken from all of the things that happened to me and my children. I look back now and can see clearer than ever that God carried me through this devastating time in my life. I just didn't know that it was Him at the time."

Some people have felt angry at God, so they chose to break faith with Him. It is understandable to want to end relationships with those we believe hurt us. It is our belief that God has been saddened by our circumstances too and desires us to bring our hurts, anger, questions, and broken hearts to Him. As we draw closer to God, He heals our broken hearts in ways no one else can.

From our observation, people can become stuck in grief because of misplaced anger or consuming bitterness. Some choose to reside in that miserable place and their choice, in turn, affects everyone around them and can cause the rest of the family to live in the same distressed state. On the other hand, for many parents, it is their faith and the love and support of their brothers and sisters in that faith that help them through the first year of grief.

Our Surprise at Jay's Memorial Service

The lights were set low as the candles illuminated the church. The organist softly played favorite melodies and the beautiful bouquets of flowers from family and friends decorated the steps and altar. Jay's memorial service was led by three pastor friends who said kind, funny, and reassuring things about Jay. The memorial service was a healing experience for our traumatized family. We anticipated that.

What we did not expect was the reception that was provided afterward. Delicious food and beverages seemed to magically appear out of nowhere. Sweet hostesses catered lovingly to the mourners. Just as efficiently, food was packed up, whisked away after the reception, and thoughtfully delivered to our house. We didn't have a clue that all of this was going to happen and we didn't even know who organized it or all of the many caring volunteers who carried it out.

Random acts of compassionate kindness, love and thoughtfulness helped us immensely during the first year. The point is, friends of faith or support groups often want to help us, to pray for us, to grieve with us, or to lend a helpful hand. To cut ourselves off from them slows down the healing process.

We can choose to hold tightly to our faith. It is true that life will never be the same for us, but it can go on to have new meaning and purpose again whether we think it can or not. Cling to the hope that faith offers because hope will ultimately not disappoint.

What Faith Can Do

A Christian Bible Study teacher for twenty-five years, Daisy Catching enjoyed a close mother-son bond. She and her husband, Dick, had their world radically changed forever when their only child, young Danny, died unexpectedly of a heart attack. Because of her spiritual anchor in Jesus, she realized the journey to healing required a tremendous effort of patience, faith and hope.

After coming to terms with Danny's death, her greatest desire was to reach out to other Christian moms going through similar anguish. She was given a vision to pass on the hope that seems elusive after the death of a child or children. She founded UMBRELLA MINISTRIES in 1996 with the sole purpose of helping mothers through the grieving process of losing a child.

Since its beginning, UMBRELLA MINISTRIES has offered comfort, encouragement, and hope to hundreds of mothers across the United States, including Alaska, and Canada.

Grieving the death of a child can be a painful and lonely struggle. This ministry assists bereaved mothers through their difficult period with support group meetings, conferences, and personal phone calls. Love and hope were given freely - all because Daisy chose to put her faith into action.

Jeff Stirling was killed instantly when he was thrown from the plane he was piloting in 1988. His mom, Linda, was enshrouded in a fog of grief. Reaching for hope, she dusted off her Bible and poured herself into its soothing words of comfort. She was strengthened and comforted as she prayed to God. Her vision, like Daisy's, was to help others find the path to joy and healing that she experienced. Daisy invited Linda to be the regional director of UMBRELLA MINISTIES. Linda then started a chapter which meets monthly in San Diego. True faith in action!

6
Softening
Special Dates

Firsts

Leena Landmark's beautiful 16-year-old daughter Lauren died on St. Patrick's Day. The following year, leading up to the first anniversary of Lauren's death, Leena took off the entire week from work. She wrote, "I didn't think that I needed to take this entire week off work. I just planned on taking the 17th off, but I can't think about anything except her death. Why do the days leading up to the date of her death hurt so much?"

All of those "firsts" after the death of our loved one are extremely difficult to face. Even after we were through the deepest part of the grieving process, throughout the year we experienced waves of grief. Like waves at the beach, some gently ebbed and flowed, others hit like a tsunami, especially those leading up to special dates like birthdays, death dates, graduations, anniversaries, or holidays. Expect that. "Special Day" reactions are normal and the intense pain will fade as the years pass, even though we can't expect it to go away completely.

You will find kindred spirits between the pages in this chapter. These kindred spirits provide insight, comfort and strength as we venture through this unfamiliar territory of the first year and beyond after a passing away of a beloved child.

Since we are all so different, each individual needs to personally determine how to handle or "soften" those special days and what works best for him or her. There is no right way to mark important dates. Other grieving parents have shared with us the following four approaches to special days in our first year. This advice also helped us in subsequent years:

- SOME CHOOSE TO <u>SLEEP</u> through the occasion in order to handle the pain.
- SOME JUST TRY TO <u>GET THROUGH</u> THE DAY by sheer determination on their child's birthday or anniversary of their death with no set plans. It's the mind over matter approach. When I was a young girl, my father would say, "Pull yourself up by your bootstraps." That meant I had to deal with it unemotionally and go on. That advice didn't work for me. And, this approach can actually be detrimental if your thoughts and feelings are kept bottled up inside.
- SOME CHOOSE TO BE <u>SPONTANEOUS</u>. When Father's Day arrives, some bereaved dads decide what they should do that very morning.
- SOME PARENTS CHOOSE TO <u>PLAN AHEAD</u>, knowing that they are likely to experience stronger emotions or reactions on those special anniversaries or holidays. They want to establish new traditions, organize get-togethers with close family or friends, or do something special to remember and celebrate their deceased loved one's life.

Don't let others pressure you on what you should or shouldn't do. Do what is helpful to you. You'll probably find yourself dreading some of those upcoming special days, fearful of being overwhelmed by painful memories and emotions. But it can be less painful if we don't expect too much of ourselves or others. In some cases, the anticipation can be worse than the reality. Realize that any anniversary, birthday, or holiday, will never be the same. We alone can determine how to face them or soften the reality of the emptiness. It can be a time for us to focus on the love that lives on, the good things about our relationship with our child, and the time we had together rather than the loss.

Reactions

For example, we have friends who said Memorial Day was "ruined forever" because their unborn baby died that day. It will always have a bittersweet feeling for that couple, but it doesn't need to be "ruined forever." Forever is a long time. They think they will never be able to celebrate that day. Whatever decision they make will in all likelihood happen. The mind is a powerful tool. The personal pain felt on certain days may not go away for some, but other bereaved parents we know, have chosen a different perspective, attitude, or plan. They have chosen to look outward and to focus on the reason for the season or holiday.

On Memorial Day, we shared our thoughts with our friends who had the choice of where their focus could be. They could choose to celebrate the people who served in the military to preserve our freedom or possibly celebrate the good memories they had in years past instead of focusing on their loss. They could choose to celebrate with the friends and family or veterans they know.

Responses

Personally, we acknowledge that celebrating Memorial Day will not be the same without the exuberant Jay leading us in silly games, or laughing as the water balloons burst, or his burning the chicken on the grill at our family picnic. Now we have chosen a new way to commemorate the day. In order to remember Jay and honor those who have died for their country, we have reached out to organizations like T.A.P.S. (Tragedy Assistance Programs for Survivors of Military Service) in order to work alongside other grieving parents. We've visited the forgotten veterans at the VA Hospital and thanked them for their service by spending time with them or signing patriotic songs for them.

Instead of looking inward at our loss, we try to make a conscious decision to look outward, to lighten someone else's loss. We like to believe we pay tribute to our loved ones when we do things in their name. Some years are easier than others.

One of the toughest "firsts" for me to face was Jay's birthday when I realized it wouldn't be the same without our fun-loving Jay to lead the way in merry making. I dreaded the day months in advance and didn't like the negativity I could see that was brought to others around me. I wanted to do something positive, anything to help me get out of the "funk." So, as that first birthday approached, we came upon what we considered a brilliant idea – create Jay's Memorial Garden as a little sanctuary on the side of our house. It took much time, thought, and effort to be spent in a productive way. Step by step, we laid each brick for a little patio, put up white trellises with twinkly lights, and planted lots of colorful flowers in planter boxes. We hung a hummingbird feeder and wind chimes. Then, we purchased a lighted water fountain with three leaping dolphins since they were Jay's favorite animal. To complete Jay's Memorial Garden, we added a double rocking bench with pillows.

Jay was cremated and not buried in a cemetery, so his memorial garden is a place we can go to feel physically closer to Jay the way others get to do when they visit their deceased loved one's tombstone or cemetery plot.

Now, we can retreat to the tranquility of starlit summer evenings by simply sitting, rocking, and listening to the waterfall, surrounded by crickets serenading each other in the night. I escape to Jay's Memorial Garden to attain a sense of peace on his birthday or any other day I want to talk to him, to be angry with him for leaving us the way he did, or to simply reminisce about the good times. The tranquility of the retreat area has proved to be a wonderfully comforting stress reliever.

It took months to visualize the entire project, to draw up the plans, purchase needed items and then execute them. In retrospect, it was worth the time involved, the money spent, and the enjoyment Jay's Memorial Garden has afforded us.

My girlfriend Lori's son, Garrett, died in a terrible automobile crash a few years after Jay's death. It was only a few months after the fatal accident that Lori took me (BJ) to a local park to see the cement bench her family had bought in Garrett's honor. They had it installed on the hill overlooking the swimming pool at the high school where Garrett was on the water polo team. Lori sits there often, and especially on all the holidays, just to talk to Garrett and visit the place where he had spent so many hours swimming.

Mary's only son, Ben, died while serving overseas in the military service. To honor his life and service to our country she also volunteers at the annual TAPS Conference for bereaved parents. In Washington, D.C. Mary was instrumental in bringing our LOVE IN MOTION Signing Choir to serve at the conference for seven years. It felt better to Doug as a grieving dad, to be a small part of serving other grievers than it did to grieve alone at home.

One year, on the anniversary of Jay's death, we held a rock ceremony and invited friends and family who were available to come. Old Testament scriptures explain the tradition of piling up rocks as a memorial to remember God's blessings. Each person who came to our rock ceremony brought a good-sized rock to build the memorial next to Jay's water fountain. After Doug read the scriptures, all of us thanked God for the time we had Jay and the blessing he had been in our lives.

Another selfless way to honor a precious child on his or her birthday or any other special days is to make a donation to a charitable organization in the child's name. Alice Felder did by planting trees in Israel in honor of her loved ones. Some people donated flower buds or flower arrangements to be placed on the altar at church. Other friends donated money toward a plaque, a tile, or a brick for a building project, or gave of their time or talents for a community fundraiser.

There are ways to remember our loved ones without spending money. We love to serve at The Compassionate Friends Conferences in Jay's memory and volunteer our time for other worthwhile causes. We feel fulfilled doing something for someone else in Jay's name because it is one way to bring honor to the name of our deceased son.

Jay, with his constant companion and beloved pet, a Siberian husky named Cabo, headed for Dog's Beach in Coronado to romp in the waves every chance they could. We've spent hours walking the same beach or splashing in the waves with Cabo since we inherited him after Jay's death. Cabo continued to miss his original master. This grandma and her "grand puppy" was found on many weekends just sitting and watching the ocean waves pulsate into the shore. Each time we went, we smiled as we remembered how much Jay loved being at the beach with Cabo.

Sometimes we've kept sweet memories alive by driving past the places where Jay lived or went to school. Sometimes we met with his friends or attended their celebrations and enjoyed hearing their funny stories about Jay.

Some people find it healing to attend a public memorial service or ceremonies that mark the anniversary of trage-dies, and disasters that have claimed multiple lives. These kinds of ceremonies draw together people who have experienced loss and allow them to share experiences with others who can relate to their grief.

We advise you to be proactive in making a personal plan to do whatever helps you soften the impact of your special days.

Hindsight

Hindsight is a good teacher. If I (BJ) had to relive those first special dates over again since Jay died in 1995 (I pray I will not ever have to), I would approach them differently, utilizing some of the following bits of wisdom gleaned over time:

1. **I Would Not Expect Everyone To Remember** Jay's birth date or death date like I do. I see now how I set myself up for feeling more disappointment or failure. Those dates cannot possible mean as much to other people as they do to his own mother. It is not fair on my part to expect that.
2. **I Would Voice My Thoughts Or Concerns** that Jay's birthday or "birth into heaven" date was coming up and that I was feeling fragile or sad or lonely. It has not been fair of me to want people to "read my mind" and guess why I'm blue. Personally, I don't know any mind readers, and don't think I will ever know any. It would have been more appropriate for me to tell those I wanted to share my heart with. I would have saved me more grief when they didn't remember.
3. **I Would Have Planned Special Things** for those special days instead of thinking that I should sit at home by myself and cry. A walk on Jay's favorite beach at sunset with a friend, or a picnic at Jay's favorite park with some of his friends would have helped me remember some of the good times instead of focusing on the bad.
4. **I Would Have Done Something Nice** for someone who was feeling lonely or sad or didn't have a friend - a trip out to lunch or to a movie.

5. **I Would Have Focused More On The Good Memories** instead of the hurtful ones. When I focused on what I didn't have, it produced unhappiness and discontent. When I focused on what I did have, it produced gratitude.

6. **I Would Have Realized It Was Okay For Me To Cry** and it was okay to desire to have Jay back, even though it held me captive in selfishness. It was okay - but only for a time. I then had to make a truly hard decision to focus on helping others less fortunate. The more time I spent focused inwardly on my self and the loss of our son, the more I seemed to spiral downward into the pit of self-pity and despair. I had already spent too much time there and hated the darkness. I now know I would have helped myself recover sooner and with less stress if I had spent more time focused outwardly.

7. **I Would Have Joined A Support Group Sooner.** I would not have isolated myself from the very ones who wanted to help me. My family of origin had taught me to segregate myself from others when I was sad. However, I now believe we are made for community and for helping each other through the tough times.

A Respite Evening Out

Date night found Doug whisking me off to our favorite restaurant and theater on Coronado Island. Once our tummies were content, we strolled leisurely to our final evening destination, soaking in the beauty of a romantic, starry, full-moon sky. The award winning Lamb's Players were presenting one of their final performances of Steel Magnolias and it was to be the highlight of a long needed and wonderful evening together.

As the lights came up in the dark theater, six talented actors took their places. The set was creatively decorated like a 1980's beauty parlor. The classic play took on a distinctive sense of Louisiana with exaggerated, but believable, characters speaking with southern accents.

The enjoyment of each other, a delicious meal, and an excellent production with plenty of good clean humor produced a romantic evening we thought would continue. But, the final scene took an unanticipated turn and so did our stomachs.

In the final scene, the mother of the main character, tried to act brave before her group of life-long beauty parlor friends. Unexpectedly, she revealed that her daughter had tragically died. Because the lead actor's breakdown into a puddle of tears, lamenting, and wailing out unanswerable questions, was such a realistic portrayal, we were instantly transported back fifteen years. Vivid memories and unexpected tears ambushed both of us quicker than a flash flood. Caught up in the realism of the play, our happy, stress-free evening had twisted into an instant distressing flashback of our own actions following Jay's death.

The poignant play depicted many of the difficulties we parents face:

- Friends who do not know what to say;
- Friends who say our child is better off in heaven and the anger of a mother who hears those empty words when she is in the depths of grief;
- The often rapid mood changes in a parent struggling with grief.

- People who want to avoid the subject and other people gushing with stories of the child;
- Laughing at the funny things our child did, then crying in the same sentence as she realized there would be no more fun or funny times with the child;
- Despair at having lost the most precious gift in life.

There is an exhaustion that comes from processing all those emotions in a short period of time. It saddened us to realize similar reminders could unexpectantly materialize the rest of our lives. We never know when an event will carry us back to the early days of the heart and stomach wrenching grief we thought we had long since conquered.

Reminders Are Everywhere

Reminders aren't just tied to the calendar. They can be anywhere — in sights, sounds, touch, or smells. You might catch a glimpse of someone that looks like your child, or hear your child's favorite song, or smell fragrances and foods that remind you of your loved one. Expect the unexpected reminders because they do happen.

Another death in the family or in the news, even that of a stranger, can cause us to relive our own grief. I can't help being drawn to screaming silence and feeling a gut-wrenching stab in the heart each time we drive over the Coronado Bridge where Jay jumped to his death.

If we're unaware of those possibilities, those little surprises can ambush us suddenly, flooding us with uncontrollable emotions-even years after a loss. It is normal to feel sadness and pain when we're confronted with reminders.

Some things that help us: knowing ahead of time we can expect unexpected triggers and knowing that, because our love was deep, we can expect our pain and sorrow to be deep. Knowing this somehow helps to soften their unwanted impact.

Holidays Are Difficult

Missing You At Christmas Time
By Louise Lagerman

Every body's rushing round full of festive cheer
But I'm finding all I want to do at Christmas is come here
To talk to you a little while and bring a flower or two
I can't buy you presents now so what else can I do?
Remember my child I love you, I'm still hurting with all this pain
I don't think it'll ever stop 'til I'm with you once again.
I'm missing you at Christmastime
I'm missing you all the time.

Offers of Help

A lesson we learned during our first year of survival was to let friends give what they offer. It may be to sit with you, to share a meal, to run errands, to listen to your heartbreak. Don't be afraid, however, to tell people when you need to be alone for a time. When you feel the times of being alone are unbearable, call those who have offered help, hugs, or homemade chicken noodle soup.

Friends say "Let me know how I can help?" and most are sincere. By accepting their offers to help, friends have an opportunity to share our burden. It is okay to tell them what we want or need. On the other hand, if we don't let them help, we send the message that we're doing fine without their help, or that no help is wanted, or that future offers may even be an intrusion. Accepting their offers graciously completes the act of giving.

I felt helpless for months. So did my well-meaning friends. Sometimes I didn't even know what I wanted. I looked to others to fill in the things that needed doing. We accepted their offers to clean our house. We welcomed help with yard work and gardening, allowing those with green thumbs to bring their gardening tools and "dig in.". For those who liked to cook and offered to bring a meal, we gladly accepted.

We can look back with gratitude to friends who reached out even when we didn't know what to ask from them. When we were able to voice our needs, they were grateful for the direction and were able to serve us with confidence.

Wrap-Up of Part 2
As we survive the thaw of winter and learn to thrive in the warmth and beautiful colors of spring, we are reminded of the beauty given to us by Jay. His joy, his laughter and his love will forever bloom in our hearts along with the flowers of spring. His contagious enthusiasm and warmth will provide us hope as we steadily, and sometimes unsteadily, move forward.

On all special anniversaries, birthdays, and holidays, we think a lot about Jay, remembering the child he was, the man he became, and how much fun he was to be around. We try to honor his life by doing the best we can with the rest of our lives. We sometimes ask ourselves the question, "Would our choices and decisions in our lives today make Jay proud of us?"

We treasure memories of Jay and allow ourselves to reminisce, get nostalgic, and be thankful for the time we had with him, even though it wasn't long enough. Whatever time we had with our departed child would never have been long enough. Sometimes we think the stories we write about Jay make him sound too good to be true. At other times we're afraid we've let the memory of our precious child fade. We really don't want either to happen.

If there is one thing we've learned, it's to reach out and connect with someone going through similar circumstances. People find hope and connection by joining local support groups that meet regularly.

Surviving special dates the first few years after the death of your child may seem like an impossible task. In some ways it's like climbing a steep mountain or navigating on a churning ocean. But it can be done. So many others have had to climb that mountain or traverse those treacherous waters and are stronger for having made it to the far shore. We want to encourage you and give you hope that it can be done. That small tender shoot of hope will grow when nurtured and fertilized.

Part 3

Entering
The Hope

"There is a time for everything,
and a season for every activity under heaven:
a time to be born and a time to die,
a time to plant and a time to uproot,
a time to kill and a time to heal,
a time to tear down and a time to build,
a time to weep and a time to laugh,
a time to mourn and a time to dance."

Ecclesiastes 3: 1-4

7
Supporting
the Bereaved

Marriage and Grieving

Doud Dwight Eisenhower was born September 24, 1917, and died of scarlet fever on January 2, 1921, at the age of three. "That was and still is the great disaster of my life—that lovely, lovely little boy . . . there's no tragedy in life like the death of a child. Things never get back to the way they were before." - President Dwight D. Eisenhower[1]

The death of a child places tremendous stress on a marriage. We had heard for many years that 80% of couples who experienced the death of a child are soon divorced. We used this information as a motivator in shaping up our marriage, to do all that was necessary to ensure that Jay's death did not drive a wedge between the two of us or between us and our son, Jeff.

An article by Wayne Loder, a bereaved dad, told us about the divorce statistics he had gathered. He and his wife Pat experienced the loss of their cherished son and daughter who were both killed in the same automobile accident. After a period of intense grieving which cut their family in half, they made the decision to be of assistance to other bereaved parents. The Loders have since gone on to head up The Compassionate Friends National Offices here in the U.S.A. It is the largest support group of its kind for bereaved parents. The staff members at the TCF offices are responsible for reaching out to newly bereaved parents as well as for providing literature and organizing yearly national conferences. Wayne's article stated that only 16 percent of all couples that experience the death of a child get divorced. Less than half of those divorced reported the death of their child as a factor in the decision to divorce, according to studies he did for TCF. We are not certain if the only couples he interviewed were the ones from that group who were already reaching out to other bereaved parents for help in their time of distress, thus saving their own marriages.[2]

Andrea Gambill, owner/editor of *Bereavement Magazine* and Bereavement Publishing, Inc. and president of her local Compassionate Friends chapter, polled TCF groups around the country. She found that the number of marriages that fail after the death of a child was a small percentage. She concluded that, if the couple had any support group to voice their grief, survival of the marriage was a good probability.[3]

What we learned and took to heart from these two articles is that it doesn't matter if we are a dad or a mom, a birth parent or a step parent – we need to talk to someone as we mourn. All parents need to process their grief in a community of good listeners and be able to talk as much as needed for as long as needed, in order to get through one of the most emotionally engulfing periods we will ever have to endure. If both husband and wife can attend a grief group together, the marriage will be strengthened.

Grieving parent Alan remarried and also became a bereaved step-parent. He married Denise, whose handsome son Sean Patrick Sullivan died tragically. Advice from this couple is to speak whatever is heavy on your heart. So many bereaved parents and grandparents suffer in silence, according to them. Sometimes we want to say our child's name and tell our stories more times than most good family and friends are willing to listen. Alan says bereaved parents need to talk to each other. Mostly we need to lose our timidity about shouting out our child's names. Alan proclaims, "I will always love you ASHLEY!!" Parents love to hear and say the name of their deceased child to keep their memory alive.

The Pact

One of the best decisions we made when Jay died was that we would not let his death drive us apart. We were determined to get through this all-consuming tragedy together as a couple and as a family. We knew the journey to find peace again would not be easy and that it might be a life-long quest. We found that patience was a top requirement. Acceptance of each other's path toward healing was essential. Sacrifices were an absolute necessity. And giving grace to each other proved to be a life and marriage saver.

In the first year after Jay's death, I (Doug) ended up doing many of the household chores that had been BJ's responsibility since the beginning of our marriage. Housekeeping is not my favorite thing, but I did all of it willingly and with a heart of service and love because I knew it was one outlet for my "fixer mentality" to assist my inconsolable wife. Okay, so it wasn't ALWAYS with a willing heart, but I did the best I could under the circumstances to be a support. I knew BJ was physically and emotionally incapable of coping with even the simplest daily tasks. I realized she would be that way for an undetermined length of time.

I (BJ) was emotionally incapacitated for an extremely long time. I can't tell you how much I appreciated Doug's efforts to fill in the gap so that I could use my limited energy to heal. We also prayed often for each other and prayed for a heart of service to help our partner and surviving son when possible. It was a tremendous blessing to have a spouse who was willing to go so far above and beyond. If you don't have that support, you might be able to find your new best friend and supporter at your local bereaved parents meeting.

An article we read at the time of Jay's death stated the importance of looking for _big things_ we can do to love our spouse through a season of grief. We tried to be sensitive to the big ways we could help one another, but found it to be even more important to look for the _little things_ we could do each day that would help nurture our marriage.

We worked on developing good listening and communication dynamics before Jay died. It helped us during the mourning period because we knew we were always there for each other when one needed to talk or needed a sympathetic shoulder to cry on. The unity of our marriage was important to us before Jay's death and we made it an even higher priority after his death. We vowed to meet it head on together, thinking we would probably face new emotional strains to a degree not previously experienced.

Marital Strain and Different Choices

A grandmother was driving her teenaged grandson when their car veered off the road and rolled. He died instantly. She survived physically. Emotionally, she will never be the same. The parents of the teen were in a marriage that was not on solid ground before the tragedy. We reached out to them, hoping our similar experiences of grieving the loss of a child might in some small way comfort them. The wife welcomed our friendship and hugs, but the husband rejected our attempts to walk alongside them on their journey. The husband had made a decision that his grief was too personal and he was determined not to talk about it with anyone. He believed it was better not to dwell on the pain, but to cut his losses and move on.

She, on the other hand, joined our Bible Study group and welcomed help from several sources: family, close friends, other bereaved parents, and a support group called the Jenna Druck Foundation. Jenna was the twenty-one-year-old daughter of Ken Druck, Ph.D. Jenna was killed in a bus accident in India while participating in a Semester-at-Sea program. Dr. Druck turned his heartbreak into the creation of the Jenna Druck Foundation. Its mission is to "turn grief into hope and strength into leadership." Our new friend continued to work through her grief while her husband seemed stuck in a quicksand pit of anger. Within three years, their marriage ended when he followed through on his threat to cut his losses and move on. After the divorce, the mom had to grieve the loss of her only son and her twenty-five year marriage. In spite of climbing what seemed like an impossibly high mountain, she persevered to go on to earn a Master's degree in grief counseling and has helped many other parents at the Jenna Druck Foundation. She is another example of turning tragedy into triumph.

"Grief with purpose is an awesome force," says bereaved parent Maria Housden, author of *Hannah's Gift*. "We are the only ones who can choose whether we let our tragic circumstances make us bitter or better." Maria had always dreamed of being a writer, but life and raising a family were more important to her after Hanna was born. After Hannah's death, she followed her dream and has become a successful bestselling author.

Because we are all unique individuals, each of us will work through the dark days of mourning in our own way, in our own time, and at our own pace. Some of us have to take it one day at a time and some one hour at a time. Others deal with their loss moment by moment. Your unique personality, coupled with the relationship you had with your child and the manner in which he or she died, will dictate the length, depth, and outcome of your own journey.

"Just as the rough, hard sand creates a pearl in the oyster,
Just like it requires a downpour to produce a rainbow,
Just as the crashing waves smooth the rocks to perfection,
It takes hardship to make something beautiful."
- Anna Stanton, Age 14

What to Do

On the morning we planned Jay's memorial service, a thoughtful friend arrived at our home in time to serve us a delicious vegetable stew which she had lovingly prepared. We were grateful to receive something substantial to restore our depleted energy. We sat around the kitchen table with close family from out of state and gave thanks for the meal. We had barely begun to eat when BJ was overcome with sobbing and abruptly rose and excused herself. At this point, it was almost impossible for her to get through a meal without being ambushed by painful bouts of weeping.

Well-meaning friends and extended family sometimes felt helpless faced with the magnitude of our despair in the wake of our loss. They tried to soothe what could not be soothed. Food offerings were a welcomed practical effort. Relatives, visiting for the upcoming memorial service, needed to be fed and we were in no condition to cook or play the role of gracious hosts.

Our neglected landscaping needed tending and was efficiently taken care of by loved ones. The garbage bins mysteriously appeared at the curb on collection day and were wheeled back to the side of our house by the Garbage Fairy. Grocery store runs for more Kleenex and necessities were completed by those who offered to help in that way.

For the person wanting to lend a hand, one rule of thumb is to think of what would be helpful to you personally and then offer to do that for the grieving family, or just do it. Asking to do a specific chore gives grievers an opportunity to graciously accept your act of kindness or to suggest other things they may need.

A sweet friend of ours, Jamie, always remembers Jay's birthday and the anniversary of his birth into heaven by sending a thoughtful card or e-mail saying, "I'm praying for you as you remember Jay today." How wonderful and thoughtful it is when she lets us know that she is thinking about us on such a difficult day. We are grateful for caring friends like Jamie.

It is not always the large deeds done for someone that are remembered, but the small things done with large hearts.

To Say or Not To Say

"How could you not know something was wrong with your own son and do something?"

"How could he do such a stupid thing?"

"He's in a better place."

"Did you blame yourself?"

"How does it feel not knowing if your son went to heaven because he committed suicide?"

"I totally understand how you feel."

"When are you going to get back to your old self?"

Unfortunately, many people consciously or unconsciously, said all of these hurtful things to us in their attempts to provide comfort, but their supposed words of consolation had the opposite effect. Some people shied away altogether from our need to talk about our loss. Most people wanted to help but didn't have a clue what to do. No one in our circle of influence had experienced the death of a child or had comforted bereaved parents before.

It is those who have been through the loss of a loved one who need to educate people who haven't. We need to lovingly teach them what is appropriate to say to a grieving person. As we went through those first months of grieving, it was up to us to lovingly inform people, "Thank you for trying to comfort, but that really hurt," or "That felt warm and loving."

What is helpful to say to one griever may be hurtful to another. What is soothing to one mourner may be appalling to another. A rule of thumb is usually to offer simple, heart-felt statements without minimizing their pain.

It does not help to theorize reasons why the child died or the way it happened. Offering clichés and quoting scripture rarely help. Telling us our child is in a better place is only a painful reminder that our precious one is not here with us. Casually mentioning that we are young enough to have more children cannot fill the void left by losing this one. Saying you know how a bereaved parent feels is a hollow statement if you haven't walked in those exact shoes.

It is a good rule to try to put your self in another person's seemingly hopeless position before thoughtlessly speaking. What might be helpful or hurtful to you? If there is ever a question of how your condolence might be taken, don't say it. Generalities, minimizing the pain, and blanket statements do not help a grieving person. However, a simple "I'm so sorry" speaks volumes.

It's important to know that when a person has experienced the death of a child, they will never be the same. My well-meaning friend asked me one day, "When are you ever going to get back to being you?" Now, years later, I guess I would respond to that by saying, "I will never get back to being the "me" you once knew. I have become a new and different person with a new "normal."

We also need to remember people going through grief don't appreciate advice as much as they appreciate comfort. Never underestimate the power of listening. God gave us two ears and one mouth because we need to listen twice as much we talk. And never underestimate the power of prayer. Blanketing a friend or family member with prayer may be all you can actively do for a time. We were grateful to the people who simply offered a listening ear, a shoulder to cry on, or let us know they were praying for us.

Prayer and silence are lessons we also learned in chapter 3 of the book of Job in the Bible. After learning of the death of all ten of Job's children in a single disaster, Job's three friends came to comfort him. For a week they said nothing, they just sat with him and prayed for him. That was extremely comforting to Job. Then they opened their mouths and tried to explain why they thought this disaster happened to Job. Their words only added to Job's grief.

Henri Nouwen, wrote in *The Road to Daybreak: A Spiritual Journey*, 1990: "When we honestly ask ourselves which person in our lives means the most to us, we often find that it is those who, instead of giving advice, solutions, or cures, have chosen rather to share our pain and touch our wounds with a warm and tender hand. The friend who can be silent with us in a moment of despair or confusion, who can stay with us in an hour of grief and bereavement, who can tolerate not knowing, not curing, not healing and face with us the reality of our powerlessness, that is a friend who cares."

A book we highly recommend is *The Art of Helping* by Lauren Littauer Briggs. Guidelines in the book build a good foundation on how to be helpful and not hurtful to those we want to comfort. We give this handy paperback as a gift to those who desire to comfort friends experiencing the loss of a loved one. For those who haven't been through the experience, this book should be required reading to learn what to say and do and what NOT to say and do when a crisis hits.

The knowledge of how to properly comfort and reassure those who grieve is important for everyone since no one is exempt from experiencing loss.

Using Music as a Catalyst

My friend, Pat says, "I think every bereaved parent has one. I wish I didn't, but I do. It stops me cold in my tracks and the lump in my throat can be as big as a grapefruit. Swallowing becomes hard and tears sting my eyes. An uncontrollable force takes over my body; and I just have to go with it. I can be driving down the road, shopping in my favorite store, or sitting in a sidewalk café having a cold iced tea on a hot summer day when suddenly it happens. I hear THE SONG. Sometimes when I least expect it, they play THE SONG and memories of my precious four-year-old son, Stephen, singing along at the top of his lungs come flooding back." Oh, yes! THE SONG can have a profound impact on bereaved families, bringing on pain as acute as if we were walking barefoot on shards of glass."

Since Jay's untimely death, we Jensens have used music and movement as a means of coping when our world was turned upside down. We had been a part of *LOVE IN MOTION* Signing Choir for about five years at the time of his passing. Using sign language to sing music with this wonderful circle of friends and Bonus Family has been a great source of comfort to us. Music, and moving to that music, touches a place deep in our souls and allows us the freedom to express fragile emotions. We believe that music has been a powerful catalyst in our healing. It has soothed our grieving hearts as we have gone through the difficult and different stages of grieving.

Songs that have soothed our aching hearts as we moved through the stages of grief, range from traditional hymns to show tunes – from jazz to lullabies; oldies to newbies; country to classical to contemporary. Our preferences in music have ranged from strictly instrumentals to a particular vocalist, from choirs to rock groups. We even began to appreciate songs or musicians that drove us crazy when our Jay would blare them on his radio.. Those same songs that drove us crazy at the time have actually become significant to us.

COMPASSIONATE FRIENDS posed a question on their Facebook page that asked: *"What song has special meaning to you in relationship to your child, sibling, or grandchild who died?"* 293 people responded to the question and the songs mentioned were as varied as the people who answered. Rarely were any two songs the same. The same song may speak to an individual in different ways in different seasons of life.

Connection and reaching out to others through music started us on our way back from isolation and toward healing. It helped lift the fog of depression and kept us from dwelling on our own pain. Our *Love In Motion* Signing Choir has been invited to sign special songs at funerals for parents who have experienced the death of children. In the late nineties, we were requested to provide the music at a combined service for two little girls who were fourth grade classmates struck and killed in the crosswalk on their way home from school. Their parents requested us to present the little girls' favorite Disney songs – "A Whole New World" and "Circle of Life." We've signed "How Great Thou Art" for a mom as her soldier son in a flag draped casket was memorialized.

LOVE IN MOTION signed at little Anthony's memorial service. Anthony was a nine-year-old who was killed when his family's boat was rammed as they watched the Boat Parade of Lights in San Diego Bay. His mother asked us to sign Anthony's favorite song - the one he played over and over from his Vacation Bible School CD. "Come to Jesus" now means even more to their family after seeing it come alive visually. Music has the power to reach into the human soul and ignite a spark of hope. Using music and movement to reach out to others gave us a double blessing – first with our own healing, and second with the joy of knowing that we had made someone else's load lighter.

Any activity that helps you get through your difficult days and moments can be healing, be it music, gardening, reading, or writing.

Faith Is A Catalyst

BJ's Story
Each year as Mother's Day approaches, I have such mixed thoughts and feelings. It's not because I look back on a poor relationship with my own mother - quite the opposite. My mom was awesome! Oh, we did have our struggles and differences during my prodigal and rebellious teen years, but once I became a woman with children of my own, I could look back with nothing but admiration for a mom who selflessly and lovingly sacrificed to raise her five children.

I don't have mixed feelings about Mother's Day because our two sons gave ME a few gray hairs as they went through their own prodigal years . . . and years . . . and years! Even though they kept putting off "all that religious stuff" until they were older, I prayed fervently that my terrific boys would someday grow into terrific Christian men.

I do celebrate Mother's Day with mixed emotions every year because it is a bittersweet reminder of our devastating loss, a loss that I wish no parent would have to experience. There won't be any more, "Hi ya mom, how ya doing?" as Jay breezes into a room with his radiant smile and contagious laugher. There'll be no wedding for Jay, or children to give him gray hairs!! No grandchildren to enjoy or great grand-children through Jay.

There'll be no more Mother's Day cards like the sweet home-made one that Jay gave me on what was to become our last Mother's Day together. He wrote: "Happy Mother's Day. You're the best mom a son could ask for. I love you very much. Jay"

When we gathered for Jay's Memorial Service, our pastor delivered a very touching eulogy. He brought with him a different kind of Mother's Day card that had been kept in the files at church. I consider it the most valuable gift I could ever imagine receiving. The card had been filled out by Jay on Mother's Day 1995, and it stated: "I have accepted Jesus Christ into my heart as my Lord and Savior today."

It was only three short months later that a manically depressed Jay jumped to his death from the Coronado Bay Bridge in San Diego. His splashy entrance into heaven caused waves of questions and reexamination of priorities for family and friends. But God can bring good out of any senseless tragedy.

Jay's older brother Jeff and his best friend, Brian, were confirmed bachelors at the time of Jay's death. Neither wanted to marry or have children. Neither thought they needed God in their lives. Both were radically shaken by the loss of their lifelong friend – a little brother and best buddy. So, it wasn't long after Jay's death, that Jeff and Brian made personal decisions to invite Jesus into their lives. They realized, "Heaven wouldn't be the same without all of us there."

Brian has since married a delightful Christian lady and settled down to raise three handsome sons. Jeff married his sweetheart, Monica, who accepted Jesus as her Lord and Savior a few years later. Now, they are raising each of their three daughters to have a personal relationship with Jesus.

Life holds few guarantees and can drastically change, like ours did, in the blink of an eye. The only certainties are: one - we *CAN'T* get out of this world alive. And two - we *CAN* choose what happens to us after we die. We can choose to spend eternity in heaven when we surrender our life to God.

I don't know if you've been holding back on "all that religious stuff" until you're older, but why wait for someday? <u>TODAY</u> is the best day in this uncertain world, to make a life-changing decision that will last for all eternity. Believe me, it's the most incredible gift you could ever give or receive.

All you have to do is to be sorry for all your bad choices or wrongs and ask your Heavenly Father for forgiveness. Then you can start fresh by inviting Jesus to come into your heart and help you make better choices in the future. He is waiting to be an active part of your life.

And when you do invite Jesus into your life, be sure to share it with someone. Don't make us wait for your funeral or until we're in heaven for us to learn about it.

Even though I do experience mixed feelings about Mother's Day because of the deep heartache over Jay's death, I also feel an abundance of hope, profound joy, and a peace that passes all understanding, knowing I will see Jay again, some-day. That knowledge is why we can see light at the end of our long tunnel and be optimistic about the not- so-distant future horizon.

Doug's Story
For me (Doug), faith has been the foundation that has supported me and kept me from being swept away by the floodwaters of life. After Jay's death, my faith was a great comfort knowing that Jay was in the arms of Jesus and that Jesus would "wipe away every tear" from Jay's eyes (Revelation) and keep him safe until the day when we would be reunited.

For many years my heart grieved for parents who did not have a hope of resurrection for the dead, or questioned whether their child was in heaven. Then one Sunday, Pastor Bruce told this true story:

During World War II, three young American soldiers were fighting in the Battle of the Bulge in Belgium. One of the men died and his two buddies wanted to give him a proper burial. They went to a church in a small village and asked the young priest if their friend could find his resting place in the church's cemetery. The priest asked if the deceased man was Catholic. They said no. The priest apologized and said that, because of the rules of his church, he would not be able to bury the soldier in their cemetery because the man was not considered a believer. As they dejectedly turned to leave, the priest spoke again, offering to bury their friend just outside the cemetery fence. The two soldiers reluctantly agreed. After the priest said a few words of respect for the dead, their friend was interred just outside of the cemetery.

Many years after the war ended, the two friends were together and reminiscing about old war stories. They decided to take a trip to France to connect one last time with their departed friend. After arriving at the small village and church, they searched for their friend's grave marker outside the cemetery fence but could not find it. They entered the church to inquire and were greeted by an elderly priest. On listening to their story, the priest said he remembered their friend. The priest had been a young man, new to the pastorate of the church at the time, and it was he who had helped bury their friend. He offered to help them find the monument. He led them into the cemetery and showed them their friend's burial place. The two men were confused because they distinctly remembered the priest burying their friend outside the fence because he was not a believer. The priest stated that their friend had been buried outside the cemetery fence, but the priest had been inspired because of their love for their friend. He followed the rules about cemetery burials that had been established by his church, but noted there were no rules regarding the fence. A short time after the funeral, the priest had moved the fence to include their friend in the church's cemetery.

Our pastor concluded his story by adding that man has his beliefs about where the dead will spend eternity, but a loving God can move the fence.

As a man of faith I am convinced by many passages in the Bible that we can be certain we will spend eternity in heaven with God and our loved ones by believing that Jesus died for our sins and accepting God's free gift of salvation. I also believe, based on the Bible, that God is a loving and inclusive God who wants no one to miss the incredible joys of a heavenly eternity. If you are a believer and your child was not known to be a believer, then I encourage you to trust in God's love for you and your child. God knows you want to be reunited with your child someday and to experience all the joy that reunion will bring. None of us knows what happened in the silence of our child's heart and mind just moments before he or she breathed the last breath on this earth. Perhaps they asked God for help and He accepted their plea and carried them into His loving arms. God can move the fence.

For those who have not yet trusted God with your eternal destination, know that God loves you and has a plan for your life, both here on earth and in the life to come. God knows the pain you suffer as a bereaved parent. He too suffered at the death of his Son Jesus. He wants to reunite you with your loved one in eternity. Trust Him now. Ask Him right now to show you His love for you and for your child. Trust in Him. God can move the fence!

Reaching Out is a Catalyst

Groups, organizations, and legislative measures have been started to help other families find hope. Iris and Joe Lawly's son died in a hospital in England after he had suffered a brain injury accident. They were introduced by the hospital chaplain to Bill and Joan Henderson whose son Billy was in the same hospital and died after a long battle with cancer. This chaplain felt unable to minister to the deep grief the parents were facing but he realized that the two sets of parents could minister to one another and give comfort like no other. Realizing what a blessing it was to relate to other parents in similar situations, these two families reached out to others who had lost a child to death. These two couples formed THE COMPASSIONATE FRIENDS (TCF) in 1968 which has since grown to become the largest support group in the world for bereaved parents.

The twenty-third annual TCF International Conference, held in Arlington, VA, had just finished. Hotel personnel were stacking the 1500 chairs to clear the room for the next scheduled event at that busy hotel. Doug and I were gathering our belongings and packing a 16" x 20" sized picture of Jay that we had used as part of our choir's presentation during closing ceremonies. We thanked God that eighteen of our choir members had the opportunity to serve the attendees and prayed that our performance would touch and bring hope and healing to the hundreds of newly bereaved parents at the conference.

As the director of LOVE IN MOTION Signing Choir, careful consideration has always been given to the songs our choir presents. Six months earlier, following a week of prayer about what songs to take to the 2010 TCF Conference, two songs were laid on my heart to interpret, teach, and present at the closing ceremonies. The inspired songs were "To Where You Are" sung by Josh Groban and Charlotte Church and "I Hope You Dance" sung by LeeAnn Womack.

As Doug and I headed for the door, an obviously distraught man named Fred approached us to share his amazing story. He had been struggling with the death of his beautiful seventeen-year-old daughter two years earlier. He had awakened in a distressed state at 3:00 a.m. that morning and restlessly tossed and turned and prayed fervently for a sign from God that she was doing all right.

He said that, without a doubt, God answered his prayer when LOVE IN MOTION signed not just one, but both of his daughter's favorite songs! The meaningful songs that we were inspired to present at the closing of the conference were the same two they had chosen to use for her memorial service two years earlier.

His tears of sincere gratitude and warm bear hugs drew us into his joy. And the miracle continued to delight us when we discovered each other's children's names. Fred said he felt confident his beautiful daughter, Morgan, was joyfully dancing in heaven with our handsome son John Jay Morgan.

Turning Tragedies into Hope

A young woman went to her mother lamenting about how things were too difficult for her since her baby had died of SIDS. She did not know how she was going to make it. She was tired of struggling with the continuous agony and wanted to give up.

Her empathetic and grieving mother took her to the kitchen, filled three pots with water and placed each on a high fire. Soon the water came to a boil. In the first pot of boiling water she placed carrots, in the second she placed eggs, and in the last she placed ground coffee beans. After twenty minutes, she turned off the burners. She fished out the carrots and placed them in a bowl. She pulled out the eggs and placed them in another bowl. Then she ladled the coffee from the third pot and placed it in a third bowl. Turning to her daughter, she questioned, "What do you see?"

'Carrots, eggs, and coffee,' she replied.

Her mother asked her to feel the carrots. She did and noted that they were soft. The mother then asked the daughter to take an egg and break it. After pulling off the shell, she observed the hardboiled egg. Finally, the mother asked her daughter to sip the coffee. The daughter smiled as she smelled its sweet aroma and tasted its rich flavor. The daughter, suspecting it was a teachable moment for her mom asked, 'What does it mean?'

Her mother explained that each of these objects had faced the same adversity - boiling water, but each had reacted differently. The carrot went in strong, hard, and unrelenting. However, after being subjected to the boiling water, it softened and became weak. The egg had been fragile. Its thin outer shell had protected its liquid interior, but after enduring the boiling water, its inside became hardened. The ground coffee beans had changed the water.

With a soft and tender look, she lovingly asked her daughter, "When such horrendous adversity knocks on our door, which will we chose to become - a carrot, an egg or a coffee bean?"

The daughter thought, "Am I the carrot that seems strong, but with pain and adversity do I wilt, become soft, and lose my strength? Am I the egg that starts with a malleable heart, but hardens with the heat? Does my outer shell look good, but on the inside am I bitter and tough with a stiff spirit? Or am I like the coffee bean which actually changes the hot water, releasing its fragrance and flavor into the very thing that brings the pain?"

Coffee Makers

How is it possible to be optimistic – to be a coffee maker when you know the worst case scenario not only can happen but already has?

An American family of four was enjoying an exhilarating time as they vacationed in France. One day, as they leisurely drove down a country road viewing the beautiful scenery, another car pulled alongside of them and, for no apparent reason, fired gun shots into their car. They were grateful their little boy and little girl were asleep in the backseat and didn't witness the disturbing experience. It wasn't until they arrived at their destination that they discovered their son had been fatally struck by one of the bullets. The parents made the unbelievable decision to donate their murdered son's organs so that others in that country might live. They also went on to inspire the establishment of the European Organ Donation Program.

TAYLOR'S GIFT is a foundation started by her parents, Todd and Tara Storch from Texas, after their teenage daughter, Taylor, died in a tragic skiing accident. As difficult as it was at the time to think about giving away her organs so that others might live, they knew Taylor would have wanted to make her life count in that way, so her parents donated five of Taylor's organs. Although they did not know who the recipients would be, they have since met three of them.

Taylor's distraught and grieving mother, Tara, had one haunting wish -- she longed to hear her beloved Taylor's heart beat one more time. Through Internet research, the parents discovered that the recipient of Taylor's heart was a nurse who was the mother of two young boys. A moving experience for us Jensens was watching the two families connect on television. The nurse recipient of Taylor's heart pulled out her stethoscope and placed it on her heart while she gave Tara the ends to listen through. Tara once again heard Taylor's heart beating in its new resting place.

Because of our own loss, we've discovered many others who are reaching out to help in a variety of situations. Parents who survived the suicide of their child became the organizers of an international program called SOS – Survivors of Suicide. In San Diego, Rex and Connie Kennemer are instrumental in raising public awareness about the rising number of suicide victims among our young people by helping to organize an annual Suicide Awareness Walk. Everything changed for Rex and Connie in November 2005 when Todd, their twenty-five-year-old son and only child, was wrenched away from them by mental illness and suicide. Since that time, they have turned their grief into advocacy by founding the Community Alliance for Healthy Minds (CAHM), which sponsors various forums and benefits utilizing music, the arts, and education.

Founding Respite Retreats for couples who've lost a child is the remarkable way that Nancy and David Guthrie have allowed God to use their own suffering to comfort others and provide help in healing. The goal of each retreat is the same. "The aim is healing," Nancy says. "Not fixing. It is wanting to move forward—not just 'move on.' We want to be a unique voice in honoring their grief but also challenging them not to stay there forever." They also are the co-hosts of the GriefShare video series, used in grief groups at more than six thousand churches nationwide.

Mitch Carmody's father died of heart disease when Mitch was only fifteen years old. At age twenty-one, his older brother died because of a progressive degenerative form of cerebral palsy. When Mitch was twenty-nine, his twin sister and her two young boys were killed in a tragic automobile accident. Less than a year later his seven-year-old son, Kelly, was diagnosed with a cancerous brain tumor. The Carmodys fought hard with all they could to save their son's life with modern medicine, holistic medicine, faith, and pointed prayers for almost two years. He and his wife sold their home and everything they owned and moved to Mexico where their son experienced a miracle healing. They soon discovered that a healing is not always a cure and their son finally succumbed to the cancer. Since that time, Mitch has dedicated his life to serving the bereaved in any way he can.

Mitch tours regularly with Alan Pedersen, songwriter, singer, bereaved dad and grief support facilitator. Together they formed TWO DADS - a ministry in honor of their children. Their concerts are called "A Day with Mitch and Alan" - a day that has helped bereaved families across the nation to navigate the dark waters of the loss of child. With hope, compassion, song, wisdom, and laughter they have touched and even changed many lives on their journey serving the bereaved. Mitch's main message is: "We CAN survive and even thrive after a significant loss in our lives."

I (Doug) found new direction, new purpose, and new hope since Jay died by going back to school at age fifty two to earn my doctorate in Biblical Studies and Biblical Counseling. Now I am assisting others through their dark valleys. It brings me great joy to help ease the plight of others as they travel through their tough-times.

We know first-hand the devastation and the need for a helping hand. After surviving the first year after the death of our beloved son, we both wanted to be able to reach out to others in their most challenging times as well as help grieving parents learn how to handle the unbearable pain. Together, we have gone on to support others in their journey of grief through counseling, leading workshops, speaking at seminars and conferences, signing poignant songs, and writing. These are just a few of the thousands of stories of bereaved parents making a difference during and after their unbearable heartaches. We are all unique individuals with unique stories. We deal with grief in many different ways. The time it takes for us to get a handle on our grief and the different paths we take are as varied as our stories. Turning grief into action is one way to cope, to start the healing process, and to find new hope.

Our Choice

When tragedy strikes, it can rob us of our sense of hope. The death of our precious children tampers with our ability to believe in the best that life can offer. Maya Angelou said, "I can be changed by what happens to me. But I refuse to be reduced by it."

We don't ever "get over" this crisis or "move on" after the death of our loved one. Instead, we "grow through it", someday trusting that the goodness of life will return and we will be a productive member of society. Instead of being captured in fear and dreading the next calamity, we can choose to hope for impending joy. We know it is difficult to think this way, but we also know it's possible because it is a choice. Our grief does not have to be a life sentence that we allow to hold us prisoner forever. We can give ourselves permission to choose the freedom to enjoy life once again and to feel it to its fullest.

9
Seizing
the Hope

ACCEPTANCE AND HOPE

The last stage to experience in the grieving process is ACCEPTANCE and HOPE. This is a stage of making a conscious decision to be at peace with the way things are. Not that we like it, not that we agree with it, not that we would ever choose it ... but that we accept the reality and finality of it. It is in this stage that we know that no amount of SHOCK and DENIAL, BARGAINING and GUILT, ANGER and BLAME, DEPRESSION and HOPELESSNESS is going to change or bring our child back.

It is during this time, or in this stage, that we begin to accept our heartbreaking loss as part of our life's journey. It's far from the reality we once knew, wanted, expected or deserved, but it is our new life story. We consciously, or sub-consciously, make a choice to go on, to find meaning in life without our beloved child, to experience purpose and joy in our lives, and to bring joy to the lives of others. It is one way to honor the memory of our loved one.

Alan Wolfelt, PhD, is a noted author, educator, and grief counselor. He is known for his compassionate philosophy and states, "With acceptance and reconciliation come a renewed sense of energy and confidence, an ability to fully acknowledge the reality of the death and a capacity to become re-involved in the activities of living."

The Bible tells us that God comforts us in all our troubles so that we may comfort others. The noblest sign of acceptance we've encountered is when grieving parents use the empty hole in their hearts as motivation to try to make the lives around them less empty.

We have written about the stages of grief to inform and encourage you on your own journey and to reassure you that you can and will get through this process in your own way and in your own time. Acknowledging and accepting your own path and pace for healing will help you acknowledge and accept the needs of other grieving friends and family members. BJ and I grieved in different ways for Jay. She, as his birth parent, was not only mourning for Jay the young man, but Jay her own flesh and blood, a part of herself. I, as his step parent, was grieving not only for Jay, but also for my wife's deep loss.

At a concert to soothe bereaved hearts, a lady tearfully conveyed, "I am still alive after the deaths of my two boys, both young healthy men who died seven years apart (2000 and 2007). I woke up one morning and realized if I survived this much gut-wrenching loss, God must have a reason for me to continue. She said she owed it to her boys to live a remarkable life and to inspire and help others who are walking the same path now.

Bereaved mom, Sandy Brosam, says, "Pain is often beyond words, but never beyond love. Sometimes you have to just stop talking and start hugging!"

Happiness Does Return

Hope gently tiptoes back into our lives when we accept the truth. Joni Eareckson Tada, wrote in *A Lifetime of Wisdom: Embracing the Way God Heals You*, 2009 "Why does God allow some of His deeply loved sons and daughters to go through trials of body and spirit? Because, if they receive that suffering with faith and joy, that supernatural chemical reaction will supercharge the message of His Son's love and the suffering one will have the privilege of a life impact that will keep echoing and echoing beyond their years."

When her only son, Captain Mark Robert Nickles, died in a military jet mishap, Rose Nickles found herself lost in horrible pain and despair. In reading every book she could find about the loss of a child, she learned that grief was not about *getting over it*. It's about *coming through it* and finding a way to deal with all that has happened by moving forward with her life. Life isn't about waiting for the storm to pass; it's about learning to dance in the rain.

One day, our dark rainy clouds of sorrow slowly started to dissipate… unexpectedly. We smile without realizing it and even experience happy moments again. We surprisingly enjoy reliving joyful memories of our child. Those uplifted feelings were startling at first to us. We felt guilty when we found pleasure in things because we didn't think we should. Then, we realized that we *could* allow laughter and happiness back into our lives. We were certainly not happy for our circumstances, but we chose to be happy *in spite of* our circumstances. We knew in our hearts that our Jay would have wanted it that way.

Richter once said, "The burden of suffering seems like a tombstone hung about our necks, when in reality, it is the weight which is necessary to keep down the diver while he is hunting for pearls."

Even though it was the most horrendous time of our lives when Jay completed the act of suicide, we both still felt God's abundant love pouring out to us and His arms gently wrapping around us to provide us comfort through family and friends. We tried to look for the momentary gifts and look forward to God's miraculous ones, too. We chose to find the pearls in suffering.

We know that things will never be "back to normal" as we once knew it. In the stage of ACCEPTANCE AND HOPE, we are resigned to decide, however reluctantly, to adopt a new normal and to move ahead. We recognize that our lives can go on to find meaning, purpose and blessings - perhaps we can even find new ways to honor our deceased.

A Gift of Hope

While we were vacationing at a timeshare resort in Talladega, Alabama (near Birmingham) one summer, the chlorine in the resort pool sent us searching for a store that carried protective swim goggles. Fortunately, there was a small sporting goods store at a local strip mall. We headed there and bingo! Two pair! One for each of us. On the way out, I felt prompted to go into a little jewelry store at the other end of the mall. This was a strange prompting for me. I hadn't set foot in a jewelry store since Doug and I had bought our wedding rings many years before. Doug urged me to follow my whimsical impulse. It was totally out of character for him to want to shop, or to want me to shop! But, since we were on vacation, had no time constraints, and were on an adventure, we light-heartedly headed for the jewelry store.

Upon entering the quaint little shop, I was immediately attracted to a turn-style display case that held a plethora of gold earrings. I certainly didn't **need** another pair of earrings. I couldn't believe how I instantly spotted an adorable pair of earrings that were shaped like dolphins swimming in a circle.

I smiled, fondly remembering how our son Jay had always been fascinated with dolphins, then felt sadness welling up as I contemplated the rapidly approaching anniversary of his death.

"Why would a store hundreds of miles from any ocean carry a pair of dolphin earrings?" I wondered out loud to Doug. It seemed "serendipitous" to me, so I rationalized why I wanted the dolphin earrings: They could be a fond reminder of Jay or a birthday present to me. Maybe they could be my reward for all the hard work I had been doing in physical therapy to recover from recent serious back surgery. Or they could simply be a vacation souvenir. When the clerk showed us the pricy sales tag, I quickly returned them to the showcase and, to Doug's great relief, instantly put the thought of purchasing them out of my mind. Realizing that we were wasting precious vacation time and daylight, we hurried back to the hotel pool to swim with our new goggles .

A peaceful night's sleep followed our vigorous workout. At dawn the next morning, blissfully semi-consciousness, I was startled awake by a familiar-sounding voice. I strained my eyes, but couldn't see where it was coming from.

"How ya doing, Mom? The unmistakable greeting shocked me because that was Jay's signature greeting whenever he came home for a visit. The voice continued, "I want you to know I'm really happy here. I want to buy the dolphin earrings for your birthday." The distinctive voice persisted, "Use the money I left in my wallet. Then, when you wear the dolphin earrings, you will be happy like I am."

Then, abruptly, the voice was gone. I was left feeling disconcerted, incredulous, and yet warmed by what had just transpired. Was I mistaken, or was it some kind of incredible gift that I had gotten to hear Jay's voice again?

I was reluctant to tell Doug about this extraordinary encounter with the voice because I wasn't quite sure myself what had happened. It was too precious, yet too unbelievable, to share. I knew Doug would question my sanity! Fighting off the urge to reveal the encounter, I inwardly struggled but resolved NOT to tell Doug. I reasoned that he would attribute it to my understandable stress at this time of year. Having made the firm decision not to tell him, I felt relieved.

At breakfast that morning, I pretended everything was normal. Of course, I didn't feel normal. Somewhere between my first bite of English muffin and sip of orange juice, the tale of the unusual experience poured out uncontrollably.

Taken aback by the outpouring and skeptical of my story, Doug carefully assessed the situation with his trained legal mind, asking me very specific probing questions. Satisfied that something miraculous had occurred, he calmly and assuredly said, "God often does amazing things in the lives of faithful followers to show them His love." My levelheaded hubby reflected that the mysterious event was not a mistake, but may have been the delivery of a special love note from God and Jay.

Then I queried, "I don't remember what happened to Jay's wallet, do you?"

Doug acknowledged that he had put the missing wallet in Jay's briefcase eight years previously and had placed the briefcase in the back of his work closet soon after Jay's death. Doug reminded me that, at the time of Jay's death, I was too inconsolable to deal with his belongings, so he had hidden them out of sight. I had not seen the contents of the wallet, nor the briefcase that had long since been covered up by business papers, packed away in the closet.

Then, my usually frugal husband suggested an extravagant plan. He wanted us to go back to the jewelry store and purchase the dolphin earrings with the understanding that, if there were any money in Jay's wallet, it would help offset the cost of the purchase. I felt loved and warmed by Doug's thoughtful gesture.

That afternoon, the day before the anniversary of Jay's death, we returned to the little strip mall jewelry store and made our golden purchase. Surprisingly, the next day, as I was wearing the beautiful earrings, I realized that for the first time in eight years I actually felt warmed, peaceful, and happy on the anniversary date of Jay's drowning.

When we returned to San Diego after our restful vacation, Doug and I headed straight for the workroom closet to look for Jay's briefcase. There it sat, concealed behind some dusty old boxes. Opening it with care and respect, we instantly spied Jay's battered brown leather wallet. After examining it, we opened the cash compartment and extracted the green bills. I held my breath as Doug counted out the money. Was it a co-incidence or God-incidence? Did this pair of bereaved parents experience one of God's unexplainable miracles? The total amount of the cash equaled the exact purchase price of the shiny gold dolphin earrings! Instant tears of gratitude stung my eyes for my miraculous posthumous birthday gift as well as the gift of hope in knowing that Jay was happy and that we would someday be reunited.

Different Strokes

The information in this book is not meant to bind anyone to a grief procedure. We all need to find our own way to heal. These ideas are options for you to discover what works best for you. Understanding the general things we have in common as we travel the road of grief can help us navigate through the healing process with our built-in GPS system. (The Go Purposely Slowly system)

Carol Lane, surviving mom of Marine Sergeant Bryon Lane wrote, "Although I don't think there will ever be a time I don't miss Bryon, I feel there is a reason I am still here. We have to continue with our lives while still including Bryon in our family's consciousness." Sandy Fox is quoted as saying, "Grief is not about getting over it. It's about coming through it and finding a way to deal with all that has happened by moving forward with my life."

After surviving the first year following the death of a dearly loved child, we can become more compassionate, empathetic, and ready to reach out and help others when they grieve. It's not our circumstances that we need to focus on, but what we do in or with our circumstances that ultimately matters.

Pastor J. Vernon McGee wrote a pamphlet titled *The Death of a Little Child*. In it is a story of sweetness and beauty which can enlighten the heart of every parent who has lost a child.

> There is a custom among the shepherd folk of the Alps. In the summertime when the grass in the lower valleys withers and dries up, the shepherds seek to lead their sheep up a winding, thorny, and stony pathway to the fertile high grazing lands. The sheep, reluctant to take the difficult pathway infested with dangers and hardships, turn back and will not follow. The shepherds make repeated attempts, but the timid sheep will not follow. Finally a shepherd reaches into the flock and takes a little lamb and places it under his arm, then reaches again and takes another lamb, placing it under the other arm. Then he starts up the precipitous pathway. Soon the mother sheep start to follow and afterward the entire flock. At last they ascend the torturous trail to green pastures.
>
> The Great Shepherd of the sheep, the Lord Jesus Christ, our Savior, has reached into the flock and He has picked up your little lamb. He did not do it to rob you but to lead you out and upward. He has richer and greener pastures for you, and He wants you to follow. Will you follow Him?

Mike MacIntosh, Chaplain at Ground Zero in New York after 9-11-01, said in his latest book, "Our broken pieces can be put back together again, and often in such a way as to build a life that's stronger, more meaningful, more exciting and abundant than the one you knew before." *When Your World Falls Apart* was written by this trauma counselor and pastor to lovingly assure us that hope is possible.

Summary of Our Journey Toward Hope

"Grief is what you think and feel on the inside after someone you love dies. Mourning is the outward expression of those thoughts and feelings". – Alan Wolfelt, Ph.D.

1. **Mourners** weave in and out of many different stages of grief in the process of healing, including: Shock and Denial; Anger and Blame; Bargaining and Guilt; Depression and Hopelessness; Acceptance and Hope. It is advisable to find people who understand what you are going through to help you on the path to hope.

2. **Grievers** may use helpful tools like music, faith, and reaching out to others as catalysts toward healing. Music might include listening, playing an instrument, dancing or moving to the beat, signing to a song, and composing. Faith might include accepting Jesus into our life, reaching out to a faith community, immersing oneself in scripture and spiritual writings. Reaching out might include joining or forming a support group in your area, contacting newly bereaved parents, or putting your set of talents, gifts, and passions into action to bring about needed change in a system. Grievers find there is hope available to those who reach for it.

3. **Survivors** like us CAN go on to find purpose and meaning in our lives and be active and productive in ways we never imagined. Survivors are the ones who believe that the devastating emotions they are experiencing are normal in an abnormal situation. They are the ones who cling to the possibility that there can be hope in a seemingly hopeless situation. Survivors are the ones who choose to become better and not bitterly or permanently detoured. They are the ones who come together to share their pain, their path, their pitfalls, and their praises.

4. **Hopeful People** know that someday we'll be able to feel the peace of knowing that our sweet and precious children will always live on in OUR hearts AND the hearts of those who knew and loved them. They are the ones who choose to live out their days as a witness, testimony, and comfort to others.

"Praise be to the God and Father of our Lord Jesus Christ, the Father of compassion and the God of all comfort, who comforts us in all our troubles, so that we can comfort those in any trouble with the comfort we ourselves receive from God."
– II Corinthians 1:3, 4

JOHN JAY MORGAN

April 20, 1965-August 23, 1995

**THE JENSENS' PARTING
WORDS OF ENCOURAGEMENT:**

God bless us all as we remember the love.

For where there is love, there is hope.

Where there is hope, there is a brighter tomorrow.

CITATIONS

1. http://en.wikipedia.org/wiki/Dwight_D._
   Eisenhower#Early_life_and_family

2. http://www.divorce360.com/divorce-articles/causes-of-di-
   vorce/general/divorce-and-death-of-a-child.aspx?artid=469.

3. http://webcache.googleusercontent.com/
   search?q=cache:ADfjcrjpKNAJ:www.sidsnetwork.org/ex-
   perts/divorse.htm+statistics+divorce+after+death+of+child
   &cd=3&hl=en&ct=clnk&gl=us

REFERENCES

Chardin, Pierre Teilhard de. The Human Phenomenon.
New York: Harper & Brothers, 1959.

Gensler, Dana. 1990. A Tribute to Lindsay Nicole Gensler.
April 5, 2011 <http://www.erichad.com/lindsay/>.

http://www.blm.gov/education/00_resources/articles/un-
derstanding_ecosystem_management/poster.htm.

Lagerman, Louise. "Missing You at Christmas Time."

McGee, J. Vernon. "Death of a Little Child." Thru the Bible
Radio Network . 31 March 2011 <www.ttb.org>.

McIntosh, Mike. When Your World Falls Apart. Victor, 2002.

Pedersen, Alan. "A Dozen Roses." 2010.

Seligman, Martin. Learned Optimism: How to Change Your
Mind and Your Life. New York: Knopf, 1990.

Tada, Joni Eareckson. A Lifetime of Wisdom: Embracing
the Way God Heals You. Grand Rapids: Zondervan, 2009.

The Bible (New International Version). Ecclesiastes 3:1-4.
Grand Rapids: Zondervan, 2008.
The Bible (New International Version). II Corinthians 1: 3,4.
Grand Rapids: Zondervan, 2008